COOK

Rice & Risotto

Elizabeth Wolf-Cohen

This is a Parragon Book
First published in 2001

Parragon
Queen Street House
4 Queen Street
Bath BA1 1HE, UK

Hardback ISBN: 0-75254-969-3
Paperback ISBN: 0-75254-991-X

Printed in China

NOTE

This book uses metric and imperial measurements.
Follow the same units of measurement throughout; do not mix metric and imperial.
All spoon measurements are level: teaspoons are assumed to be 5 ml, and tablespoons are assumed to be 15 ml.
Unless otherwise stated, milk is assumed to be full fat, eggs and individual vegetables
such as potatoes are medium, and pepper is freshly ground black pepper.

Recipes using raw or very lightly cooked eggs should be avoided by infants, the elderly,
pregnant women, convalescents, and anyone suffering from an illness.

Contents

Introduction

Rice is the staple food for a third of the world's population, featuring in the cooking of countries as diverse as China, India, South America, Spain, Portugal, Italy and Africa. It is surely the ideal food – easy to store and quick to cook, nutritious and easy to digest and, above all, delicious.

MAIN RICE VARIETIES

Long-grain white rice is milled or polished to remove the outer husk, the germ and most of the bran; the rice has a long shape and a white opaque appearance. It is sometimes called Patna rice, because it originally came from that part of India. A popular all-purpose rice, it should be light and fluffy with separate grains. Cook for 15–18 minutes by the simmering or absorption method.

Easy-cook rice is long-grain white rice that is parboiled to increase its shelf life and hardness. Parboiling before milling forces the vitamins deeper into the grain, increasing its nutritional value and its cooking time, but only slightly, to 20–25 minutes. Cook as for long-grain white rice; it is more golden than long-grain white rice.

Long-grain brown rice has been milled only to remove the inedible husk. It has a distinctly nutty flavour and a much chewier texture. A soft brown colour, it is less fluffy than long-grain white rice and takes slightly longer than white rice to cook, 35–40 minutes. It is especially good in salads as it has a firmer texture.

Basmati rice is sometimes called the Champagne or king of rice. This long-grain rice grown in India and Pakistan has a distinctive perfume, a very white colour and a slimmer grain, and is light and fluffy when cooked. It cooks quickly – 10–12 minutes by the simmering or absorption method. Brown Basmati Rice is unpolished and only has the husk removed. More nutritious, dense, chewy and aromatic, it takes a bit longer to cook, 45–50 minutes. Storage time is limited as the natural oils can become rancid.

Italian risotto rice is a superb medium-short-grain Italian rice used almost exclusively for risottos. It has a chalky line down the centre. The higher the quality, the more liquid it absorbs; up to three or four times its own volume. When cooked, it forms a creamy soupy sauce with separate grains which maintain a 'firm to the bite' texture. Look for arborio, carnaroli, roma or vialone nano; 18–20 minutes for cooking but generally 25–30 minutes in a risotto.

Spanish calaspara and la bomba rice from the area near Murcia and Valencia are superb quality medium-short-grain rices grown for paella. Substitute Italian risotto rice if you cannot find it. It cooks in about 15–18 minutes, longer in paellas, 30–35 minutes.

Pudding rice or short-grain, sometimes called Carolina rice as it used to be grown in North and South Carolina, is a short-grain or round-grain rice with a chalky appearance and bland flavour. The grains are moist and sticky on cooking – 4 tablespoons can thicken 600 ml/1 pints of milk.

Thai fragrant rice or jasmine rice is a savoury white long-grain rice used in Thai and South-East Asian cooking. It has a natural aromatic flavour and is slightly soft and sticky when cooked. Cook as for basmati, about 12–15 minutes.

Japanese sushi or sticky rice is an expensive, short-grain, absorbent, sticky rice, perfect for sushi where grains must stick together to hold a shape. The opaque, pearl-like grains are white and round or slightly elongated. It cooks in about 15–20 minutes by the absorption method; it is usually mixed with a rice vinegar-sugar seasoning and fanned to cool and create a shiny appearance.

Black sweet rice or black glutinous rice is a medium short-grain rice with a dark purple-red colour. It has a rich flavour which stands up to Asian ingredients like coconut milk and palm sugar. Used in sweet dishes, it cooks in 25–30 minutes by the absorption method. The colour will dye other ingredients and cookware.

Camargue red rice is a medium oval grain with a reddish brown colour found in the South of France. It has an earthy taste and firm chewy texture. Although it loses colour in cooking, it stands up to robust flavours. Longer cooking time of 45–60 minutes by simmering or absorption method is necessary.

Wild rice is an aquatic grass. This delicious nutty rice is now being cultivated; expensive, with high-quality long glossy brown-black grains, which 'flower' when fully cooked. Cook for 55–60 minutes by simmering or absorption or follow the packet instructions. As it is very expensive, it is now being sold packaged in combination with long-grain white or basmati rice.

OTHER RICE PRODUCTS

Ground rice and rice flour is made by milling white rice to a flour-like consistency to be used as a thickener, or in cakes, pastries, biscuits and puddings. Available in varying grades of coarseness from slightly granular to very fine; rice flour is generally the finest.

Rice Flakes are a form of flaked rice used in Far-Eastern cooking styles as a thickening agent, though they can be deep-fat fried as a garnish.

Rice Noodles, including vermicelli, rice sticks, wide rice sticks and others are dry, rice-flour based pasta, twisted into skeins. They range in size from very fine (sen mee), to about 3 mm/⅛ inch thick, like tagliatelle (sen lek), to wide, about 1 cm/½ inch (sen yaai). Rehydrate in hot water for 5–20 minutes, drain and serve or use in other recipes.

Japanese harusame noodles are very thin noodles; treat as rice vermicelli.

Vietnamese rice paper wrappers are used for spring rolls, 'wraps' or other dishes. Moistened by dipping briefly into water or spraying, they can be eaten as is, steamed or fried.

Rice paper is an edible paper made from ricelike plants. Use it in baking to prevent sticking for foods like meringues; it is very thin and brittle.

Rice vinegars are red, clear, yellow or black. Flavours range from mellow to rich and fruity. Japanese vinegar is milder than Chinese. Sake, Japanese rice wine, has a distinctive flavour; sherry can be used as a substitute.

COOKING METHODS

The cooking method and time depends on the type of rice. As a rough guide allow 2 tablespoons of raw brown rice per serving, and 50 g/2 oz for other varieties; pudding recipes will vary. Three of the most basic ways of cooking rice are as follows:

Simmering is the easiest method, but imparts the least flavour. Bring a saucepan of water to the boil. Add the rice and a pinch of salt, and return to the boil. Reduce the heat and simmer.

Absorption Method: This uses the exact amount of liquid that the rice will absorb to be tender. Put the rice in a heavy-based saucepan, add a pinch of salt, a tablespoon of oil (optional) and 1½ times the amount of cold water. Bring to the boil over high heat; then reduce the heat and simmer, tightly covered, until the liquid has been completely absorbed (see simmering method for timings). Do not uncover or stir during cooking time; uncovering lets the steam escape, altering the measured amount of liquid; stirring is even worse – it can break the fragile grains of rice, releasing the starch and making sticky rice.

Remove the pan from the heat and stand for about 5 minutes, then, using a fork, fluff into a warm serving bowl. Alternatively, after removing from the heat, uncover and place a tea towel or double thickness of kitchen paper over the rice, re-cover and stand for 5 minutes. This method lets the steam be absorbed rather than drip back into the rice, creating a drier, fluffier rice. Many cooks like to put the rice on a 'heat-tamer' or asbestos mat to create an even more gentle heat after the rice has come to the boil. If not, you may get a crusty (not burnt) layer of rice stuck to the bottom of the pan. However, for many this is the best bit – to loosen the crusty layer, place the pan on a wet towel for 5 minutes, then serve, or deep-fry it and serve as a snack!

Pilaf Method: In a heavy-based saucepan over medium-high heat, heat two tablespoons of oil or butter and gently cook a finely chopped onion or 2–3 shallots. Add the measured rice and cook, stirring frequently until the rice is well coated with the fat and is translucent. Add 1½ times stock or water, a pinch of salt, and bring to the boil, stirring once or twice. At this point, cover the surface of the rice with a round of non-stick baking parchment or foil (to prevent the liquid from evaporating too quickly) and cover tightly; reduce the heat to as low as possible. Cooking times are as for the simmering method.

Soups & Salads

Rice not only makes soups and salads more substantial, but also adds an interesting texture and flavour to the dishes.

In the following pages you will find a variety of delicious soups using rice, from the classic Risi e Bisi, flavoured with peas, parsley and Parmesan, to a hearty Chicken & Sausage Gumbo. In Barley & Brown Rice Soup, the rice adds a nutty flavour and creates a deliciously thick consistency, turning it into a warming lunch dish. Pumpkin soup has a deliciously sweet flavour which is subtly enhanced by rice, while in Prawn Bisque with Rice, rice is used as a thickener without overpowering the delicate flavour of the soup. Soups like Vietnamese Beef & Rice Noodle Soup feature rice in the form of light, delicate noodles, while a chowder is given a different twist with wild rice and smoked chicken.

On the salad front, the nutty flavour and chewy texture of wild rice work well with the smoky flavours in Wild Rice & Bacon Salad with Scallops, and add an interesting dimension to a fruity bean salsa. Red rice from the Carmargue in the South of France also has a particular nutty flavour, which is good with the spiciness of Red Rice Salad with Hot Dressing.

You can also use rice to give old favourites a lift – try green salad with toasted rice, or turn a Greek salad into a substantial meal by adding cooked rice. Gazpacho Rice Salad is just as refreshing as the classic Spanish soup it is based on, while Caesar Salad is given an exotic touch with Thai flavourings and a rice paper garnish.

Risi e Bisi

Serves 4

INGREDIENTS

900 g/2 lb fresh unshelled peas
4 tbsp unsalted butter
1 onion, finely chopped
850 ml/1½ pints chicken stock
200 g/7 oz arborio rice

2 tbsp chopped fresh flat-leaved
   parsley
60 g/2¼ oz freshly grated
   Parmesan cheese
salt and pepper

TO GARNISH
tomato slices
Parmesan cheese shavings
fresh basil leaves

1 Remove the peas from their shells – the shelled peas should weigh about 300 g/10½ oz.

2 Melt the butter in a large heavy-based saucepan over a medium heat. Add the onion and cook for about 2 minutes, stirring occasionally, until beginning to soften.

3 Add the shelled peas and cook, stirring occasionally, for a further 2–3 minutes. Gradually add the chicken stock and bring to the boil. Reduce the heat and simmer, covered, for about 10 minutes, stirring occasionally.

4 Add the rice and season with a little salt and pepper. Simmer, covered, for about 15 minutes, stirring occasionally, until the rice is just tender.

5 Stir in the parsley and adjust the seasoning. If the soup is too thick, add a little more stock. Stir in the Parmesan, then ladle into bowls.

6 Serve immediately, garnished with tomato slices, Parmesan shavings and basil leaves.

COOK'S TIP

You can substitute 300 g/10½ oz frozen peas for fresh: defrost under running hot water and cook for about 5 minutes with the stock in Step 3. Continue from Step 4.

Provençal Pumpkin Winter Soup

Serves 6

INGREDIENTS

1 kg/2 lb 4 oz fresh orange-
   fleshed pumpkin or winter
   squash, such as butternut or
   hubbard
2 tbsp olive oil
1 large onion, chopped
2 garlic cloves, chopped
2 tsp fresh thyme leaves

1.5 litres/2¾ pints chicken or
   vegetable stock,
   or water
1 bay leaf
½ tsp crushed dried chillies
100 g/3½ oz short-grain rice,
   such as arborio or valencia
1 tsp salt

300 ml/10 fl oz single cream
   or milk
freshly grated nutmeg
pepper
fresh thyme sprigs, to garnish
garlic croûtons, to serve
   (optional)

1 Remove any seeds from the pumpkin, then peel. Cut into small cubes and set aside.

2 Heat the oil in a large saucepan over a medium heat. Add the onion and cook for about 4 minutes until soft.

3 Stir in the garlic and thyme and cook for 1 minute. Stir in the pumpkin, stock, bay leaf, chillies and half the rice. Bring to the boil, skimming off any foam. Reduce the heat to low and simmer, covered, for about 1 hour until the pumpkin is very tender.

4 Meanwhile, bring a saucepan of water to the boil. Add the salt, sprinkle in the remaining rice and simmer for about 15 minutes until tender. Drain, rinse, then drain again. Set aside.

5 Working in batches, process the pumpkin soup in a blender until smooth and strain into a large saucepan. Add the cooked rice, cream and nutmeg to taste. Season with salt and pepper and garnish with thyme. Serve with croûtons, if wished.

COOK'S TIP

Cooking half the rice separately, then adding it to the puréed soup, gives the finished dish texture, but if you prefer a completely smooth soup, cook all the rice at Step 3 and blend.

Tomato & Red Rice Soup

Serves 4–6

INGREDIENTS

2 tbsp olive oil
1 onion, finely chopped
1 carrot, finely chopped
1 stick celery, finely chopped
3–4 garlic cloves, finely chopped
900 g/2 lb fresh ripe tomatoes, skinned, deseeded and finely chopped (see Cook's Tip)

1 bay leaf
½ cinnamon stick (optional)
1 tsp fresh thyme leaves or ½ tsp dried thyme
1 tsp dried oregano
1 tbsp brown sugar
½ tsp cayenne pepper, or to taste
1.5 litres/2¾ pints chicken stock or water

100 g/3½ oz red rice or long-grain brown rice
1 tbsp chopped fresh oregano leaves
salt and pepper
freshly grated Parmesan cheese, to serve

1 Heat the oil in a large saucepan over a medium heat. Add the onion, carrot and celery and cook for about 10 minutes, stirring occasionally, until very soft and beginning to colour. Stir in the garlic and cook for a further minute.

2 Add the tomatoes, bay leaf, cinnamon stick, if using, thyme, dried oregano, sugar and cayenne pepper and cook, stirring occasionally, for about 5 minutes until the tomatoes begin to cook down.

3 Add the stock and the rice and bring to the boil, skimming off any foam. Reduce the heat and simmer, covered, for about 30 minutes until the rice is tender, adding more stock if necessary.

4 Stir in the fresh oregano leaves and season with salt and pepper. Serve immediately, with Parmesan cheese for sprinkling.

COOK'S TIP

You need well-flavoured tomatoes for this soup; if unavailable, use canned Italian plum tomatoes instead, and reduce the amount of stock if the tomatoes are packed in a lot of juice.

Barley & Brown Rice Soup with Chard

Serves 4–6

INGREDIENTS

100 g/3½ oz pearl barley
100 g/3½ oz long-grain brown rice
450 g/1 lb chard, trimmed and
    soaked for 10 minutes
2 tbsp olive oil
1 large onion, finely chopped
2 carrots, finely chopped
2 sticks celery, finely chopped

2 garlic cloves, finely chopped
400 g/14 oz can chopped Italian
    plum tomatoes with their juice
1 bay leaf
1 tsp dried thyme
1 tsp herbes de Provence or dried
    oregano

1 litre/1¾ pints chicken or
    vegetable stock
450 g/1 lb can cannellini beans,
    drained
2 tbsp chopped fresh parsley
salt and pepper
freshly grated Parmesan cheese,
    to serve

1 Bring a large saucepan of water to the boil. Add the barley and the brown rice and return to the boil. Reduce the heat and simmer gently for 30–35 minutes until just tender. Drain and set aside.

2 Drain the chard. Cut out the hard white stems and slice the stems crossways into very thin strips; set aside. Roll the leaves into a long cigar shape and shred thinly; set aside.

3 Heat the oil in a large saucepan. Add the onion, carrots and celery and cook, stirring frequently, for about 5 minutes until soft and beginning to colour. Add the garlic and cook for a minute longer. Add the tomatoes and their juice, the bay leaf, thyme and herbes de Provence. Reduce the heat and simmer, partially covered, for about 7 minutes until all the vegetables are soft.

4 Stir in the sliced white chard stems and the stock. Simmer gently for about 20 minutes. Add the shredded green chard and simmer for a further 15 minutes.

5 Stir in the beans and parsley with the cooked barley and brown rice. Season with salt and pepper. Bring back to the boil and simmer for a further 8-10 minutes. Serve immediately, with Parmesan for sprinkling.

Prawn Bisque with Rice

Serves 6

INGREDIENTS

650 g/1 lb 7 oz cooked prawns, in their shell
1 stick celery, with leaves if possible, chopped
½ tsp crushed dried chillies
about 1.2 litres/2 pints water
4 tbsp butter
1 onion, finely chopped

2 carrots, finely chopped
50 ml/2 fl oz brandy or cognac
225 ml/8 fl oz dry white wine
1 bay leaf and 10 parsley sprigs, tied together with kitchen string
1–2 tsp tomato purée

1 tsp paprika
3 tbsp basmati or long-grain white rice
150 ml/5 fl oz double or whipping cream
fresh dill sprigs or long chives, to garnish

1 Peel 6 prawns, leaving the tails intact; reserve for garnishing. Peel the remainder, reserving shells.

2 Put all the shells in a saucepan, with the celery stick and dried chillies. Add the water. Bring to the boil over a high heat, skimming off any foam. Reduce the heat and simmer gently for about 30 minutes. Strain and set aside.

3 Melt the butter in a large saucepan. Add the onion and carrots and cook for about 8 minutes, stirring frequently, until the vegetables are soft. Add the brandy and, standing well back, ignite with a long match. Allow the flames to die down, then stir in the wine. Boil for about 5 minutes to reduce by about half.

4 Add the reserved stock, bay leaf and parsley stem bundle, tomato purée, paprika and rice; stir. Bring to the boil, then simmer gently for 20 minutes until the rice is very tender.

5 Remove the parsley bundle. Working in batches if necessary, process the soup in a blender and strain into a clean saucepan. Stir in the cream and simmer for 2–3 minutes. Add the 6 prawns and heat through for a minute. Ladle into 6 bowls, arranging a prawn in each serving. Garnish and serve.

Italian Chicory & Rice Soup

Serves 4–6

INGREDIENTS

450 g/1 lb heads chicory
4 tbsp butter
1 onion, finely chopped
1 litre/1¾ pints
    chicken stock

100 g/3½ oz arborio or
    carnaroli rice
freshly grated nutmeg
2–4 tbsp freshly grated
    Parmesan cheese

salt and pepper
fresh herbs, to garnish

1 Separate the leaves from the chicory, discarding any damaged outer leaves. Wash the leaves thoroughly under cold running water and drain well. Stack several leaves in a pile and roll tightly, then shred the leaves into 1 cm/½ inch ribbons and set aside. Continue with the remaining leaves.

2 Melt the butter in a large heavy-based saucepan over a medium heat. Add the onion and cook, stirring occasionally, for about 4 minutes until soft and just beginning to colour. Stir in the shredded chicory and

cook, stirring frequently, for about 2 minutes until the leaves wilt.

3 Add half the stock and season with salt and pepper. Reduce the heat and simmer, covered, over a very low heat for 25–35 minutes until tender.

4 Add the remaining stock, and bring to the boil. Sprinkle in the rice and simmer, partially covered, over a medium heat for 15–20 minutes, stirring occasionally, until the rice is just tender, yet firm to the bite.

5 Remove from the heat and season with more salt and pepper, if necessary, and nutmeg. Ladle into bowls and sprinkle with a little Parmesan. Serve immediately, garnished with herbs.

COOK'S TIP

Long-grain white rice can be substituted for arborio or carnaroli, but the round rice is slightly more starchy.

Turkey & Rice Soup

Serves 8–10

INGREDIENTS

1 onion, finely chopped
2 carrots, diced
200 g/7 oz long-grain white rice
2 leeks, thinly sliced
225 g/8 oz frozen peas
115 g/4 oz fresh or frozen
  (defrosted) mangetout, thinly
  sliced
115 g/4 oz fresh spinach or
  watercress, washed and
  shredded

450 g/1 lb cooked turkey meat,
  diced
1 tbsp finely chopped fresh
  parsley
salt and pepper

STOCK
1 bunch fresh parsley
2 turkey legs

1 bay leaf
1 tsp dried thyme
2 onions, unpeeled, cut into
  quarters
2 carrots, cut into chunks
2 sticks celery, cut into chunks
1 parsnip, cut into chunks
  (optional)
1 dessert apple or pear (optional)
1 tbsp black peppercorns

1 To make the stock, first tie the parsley sprigs into a bundle, then put in a large pan with the remaining stock ingredients and enough cold water to cover by 2.5 cm/ 1 inch.

2 Bring to the boil, over a high heat, skimming off any foam. Boil for 2 minutes, then reduce the heat to low and simmer very gently for 2–3 hours. Cool the stock

slightly, then strain into a large bowl. Skim off any fat from the surface, then wipe a piece of kitchen paper across the surface.

3 Put about 3 litres/ 5¼ pints of the turkey stock in a large saucepan. Add the onion and carrots and bring to the boil.

4 Add the rice, reduce the heat and simmer for

15–20 minutes until the rice is tender, stirring once or twice.

5 Stir the remaining vegetables into the pan of soup and simmer for 10 minutes. Add the cooked turkey meat, heat through and season with salt and pepper. Stir in the parsley and serve.

Wild Rice & Smoked Chicken Chowder

Serves 6–8

INGREDIENTS

75 g/2¾ oz wild rice, washed
3 fresh corn-on-the-cobs, husks
     and silks removed
2 tbsp vegetable oil
1 large onion, finely chopped
1 stick celery, thinly sliced
1 leek, trimmed and thinly sliced

½ tsp dried thyme
2 tbsp plain flour
1 litre/1¾ pints
     chicken stock
250 g/9 oz boned smoked
     chicken, skinned, diced
     or shredded

225 ml/8 fl oz double or
     whipping cream
1 tbsp chopped fresh dill
salt and pepper
fresh dill sprigs, to garnish

1 Bring a large saucepan of water to the boil. Add a tablespoon of salt and sprinkle in the wild rice. Return to the boil, then reduce the heat and simmer, covered, for about 40 minutes until just tender, but still firm to the bite. Do not overcook the rice as it will continue to cook in the soup. Drain and rinse; set aside.

2 Hold the corn cobs vertical to a cutting board and, using a sharp heavy knife, cut down along the cobs to remove the kernels. Set aside the kernels. Scrape the cob to remove the milky juices; reserve for the soup.

3 Heat the oil in a large pan over a medium heat. Add the onion, celery, leek and dried thyme. Cook, stirring frequently, for about 8 minutes until the vegetables are very soft.

4 Sprinkle over the flour and stir until blended. Gradually whisk in the stock, add the corn with any juices and bring to the boil; skim off any foam. Reduce the heat and simmer for about 25 minutes until the vegetables are very soft and tender.

5 Stir in the smoked chicken, wild rice, cream and dill. Season with salt and pepper. Simmer for 10 minutes until the chicken and rice are heated through. Garnish with dill sprigs and serve immediately.

Chicken & Sausage Gumbo

Serves 6–8

INGREDIENTS

1.25 kg/2 lb 12 oz chicken, cut
   into 8 pieces
85 g/3 oz plain flour
175 ml/6 fl oz vegetable oil
700 g/1 lb 9 oz andouille (Cajun
   smoked sausage), Polish
   kielbasa or other smoked pork
   sausage, cut into 5 cm/
   2 inch pieces
2 large onions, finely chopped
3–4 sticks celery, finely chopped

2 green peppers, deseeded and
   finely chopped
700 g/1 lb 9 oz okra, stems
   trimmed and cut into 1 cm/
   ½ inch pieces
4 garlic cloves, finely chopped
2 bay leaves
½ tsp cayenne pepper, or to taste
1 tsp ground black pepper
1 tsp any dry mustard powder
1 tsp dried thyme

½ tsp ground cumin
½ tsp dried oregano
1.5 litres/2¾ pints chicken stock,
   simmering
3–4 ripe tomatoes, deseeded
   and chopped
salt
400 g/14 oz long-grain white
   rice, cooked, to serve

1 Toss the chicken in about 2 tablespoons of the flour. Heat 2 tablespoons of the oil in a large frying pan. Add the chicken and cook for about 10 minutes until golden. Set aside.

2 Add the sausage pieces to the pan, stirring and tossing, for about 5 minutes until beginning to colour. Set aside.

3 Heat the remaining oil in the cleaned-out pan until just beginning to smoke. Add the remaining flour all at once and whisk immediately to blend into the oil. Reduce the heat and cook, stirring, for about 20 minutes until the roux is a deep rich brown.

4 Add the onions, celery and peppers to the roux and cook, stirring frequently, for about 3 minutes until beginning to soften. Stir in the okra, garlic, bay leaves, cayenne pepper, black pepper, mustard powder, thyme, cumin and oregano and stir well.

5 Little by little, whisk the hot stock into the mixture, stirring well after each addition. Simmer for about 10 minutes. Stir in the tomatoes and the reserved sausage and chicken pieces and simmer for about 20 minutes until the meat is tender.

6 To serve, fill a cup with rice, packing it lightly, then unmould into the centre of a wide soup bowl. Spoon the gumbo around the rice.

Vietnamese Beef & Rice Noodle Soup

Serves 4–6

INGREDIENTS

175 g/6 oz packet dried rice stick
  noodles
4–6 spring onions, sliced thinly
  on the diagonal
1 fresh red chilli, sliced thinly on
  the diagonal

1 bunch fresh coriander
1 bunch fresh mint
350 g/12 oz fillet or rib eye steak,
  very thinly sliced
salt and pepper

STOCK
900 g/2 lb meaty beef bones
4 spring onions, chopped
2 carrots, cut into chunks
1 leek, cut into chunks
3 whole star anise
1 tsp black peppercorns

1 To make the stock, put the beef bones, spring onions, carrots, leek, star anise and peppercorns in a large saucepan or flameproof casserole and bring to the boil, skimming off any foam. Reduce the heat and simmer gently, partially covered, for about 3 hours.

2 Strain into a large bowl and skim off any fat; draw a piece of kitchen paper across the surface to remove any drops of fat.

3 Cover the noodles with warm water and leave for 3 minutes until just softened; drain the noodles. Using scissors, snip the noodles into 10 cm/4 inch lengths.

4 Arrange the spring onions and chilli on a serving plate. Strip the leaves from the coriander stems and arrange in a pile on the plate. Strip the leaves from the mint stems and arrange in a pile next to the coriander leaves.

5 Bring the beef stock to the boil in a large saucepan. Add the noodles and simmer for about 2 minutes until tender. Add the beef strips and simmer for about 1 minute. Season to taste.

6 Ladle the soup into bowls and serve with the spring onions, chilli and herbs handed separately.

Warm Greek-style Rice Salad

Serves 4–6

INGREDIENTS

200 g/7 oz long-grain white rice
80 ml/3 fl oz extra-virgin olive oil
2–3 tbsp lemon juice
1 tbsp chopped fresh oregano or
   1 tsp dried oregano
½ tsp Dijon mustard
2 large ripe tomatoes, deseeded
   and chopped

1 red or green pepper, deseeded
   and chopped
75 g/2¾ oz Kalamata or other
   brine-cured black olives,
   stoned and halved
225 g/8 oz feta cheese, crumbled,
   plus extra cubes, to garnish
1 tbsp capers, rinsed and drained

2–4 tbsp chopped fresh flat-
   leaved parsley or coriander
salt and pepper
diced cucumber, to garnish

1 Bring a saucepan of water to the boil. Add a teaspoon of salt and sprinkle in the rice; return to the boil, stirring once or twice. Reduce the heat and simmer for 15–20 minutes until the rice is tender, stirring once or twice. Drain and rinse under hot running water; drain again.

2 Meanwhile, whisk together the olive oil, lemon juice, oregano, mustard, and salt and pepper in a bowl. Add the tomatoes, pepper, olives, feta cheese, capers and parsley and stir to coat in the dressing. Leave to marinate.

3 Turn the rice into a large bowl; add to the vegetable mixture and toss to mix well.

4 Season the salad with salt and pepper to taste, then divide between 4–6 individual dishes and garnish with extra feta cheese cubes and diced cucumber. Serve just warm.

VARIATION

This salad is also delicious made with brown rice – just increase the cooking time to 25–30 minutes.

Wild Rice & Bacon Salad with Scallops

Serves 4

INGREDIENTS

150 g/5½ oz wild rice
600 ml/1 pint water or more if
   necessary
50 g/1¾ oz pecans
   or walnuts
2 tbsp vegetable oil

4 slices smoked bacon,
   diced or sliced
3–4 shallots, finely chopped
80 ml/3 fl oz walnut oil
2–3 tbsp sherry or cider vinegar
2 tbsp chopped fresh dill

8–12 large scallops, cut
   lengthways in half
salt and pepper
lemon and lime slices, to serve

1 Put the wild rice in a saucepan with the water and bring to the boil, stirring once or twice. Reduce the heat to low, cover, and simmer gently for 30–50 minutes, depending on whether you prefer a chewy or tender texture. Using a fork, fluff the rice into a large bowl; let cool slightly.

2 Meanwhile, toast the nuts in a frying pan for 2–3 minutes until just beginning to colour, stirring frequently. Cool and roughly chop; set aside.

3 Heat a tablespoon of the vegetable oil in the pan. Stir in the bacon and cook, stirring occasionally, until crisp and brown. Transfer to kitchen paper to drain. Remove some of the oil from the pan and stir in the shallots. Cook for 3–4 minutes, stirring from time to time, until soft.

4 Stir the toasted nuts, bacon and shallots into the rice. Add the walnut oil, vinegar, half the chopped dill and salt and pepper to taste. Toss well to combine the ingredients, then set aside.

5 Brush a large non-stick frying pan with the remaining oil. Heat until very hot, add the scallops and cook for 1 minute on each side until golden; do not overcook.

6 Divide the wild rice salad among 4 individual plates. Top with the scallops and sprinkle with the remaining dill. Garnish with a sprig of dill, if desired, and serve immediately with the lemon and lime slices.

Spicy Rice, Bean & Corn Salad

Serves 4–6

INGREDIENTS

100 g/3½ oz long-grain white or brown rice	1 fresh red or green chilli, deseeded and finely chopped	2 tbsp chopped fresh coriander
3 corn-on-the-cobs	1 tbsp lemon juice	400 g/14 oz can butter beans
groundnut oil	1 tbsp lime juice	115 g/4 oz sliced cooked ham, diced
1 small red onion, finely chopped	½ tsp cayenne pepper, or to taste	salt and pepper

1 Bring a saucepan of water to the boil. Add a teaspoon of salt and sprinkle in the rice. Return to the boil, stirring once or twice. Reduce the heat and simmer for 15–20 minutes until the rice is tender. (Brown rice will take 25–30 minutes.) Drain and rinse under cold running water; drain and set aside.

2 Scrape down each corn cob with a knife to remove the kernels; set aside. Scrape along each cob to remove the milky residue and transfer to a small bowl.

3 Heat 1 tablespoon of the oil in a saucepan. Add the corn kernels and cook gently for about 5 minutes, stirring frequently, until tender. Add the red onion and chilli and stir for about 1 minute until blended. Transfer to a plate and let cool slightly.

4 Place the lemon and lime juices in a large bowl and whisk in the cayenne pepper, 2–3 tablespoons of oil and the milky corn liquid. Whisk in the chopped coriander until well combined.

5 Using a fork, fluff in the cooked rice and corn and onion mixture. Add the beans and ham and season with salt and pepper. Transfer to a serving bowl and serve immediately.

COOK'S TIP

Although fresh corn-on-the-cob has a delicious flavour, you could substitute canned or defrosted frozen corn kernels without any problem.

Gazpacho Rice Salad

Serves 4–6

INGREDIENTS

125ml/4 fl oz extra-virgin olive oil

1 onion, finely chopped

4 garlic cloves, finely chopped

200 g/7 oz long-grain white rice or basmati

350 ml/12 fl oz vegetable stock or water

1½ tsp dried thyme

3 tbsp sherry vinegar

1 tsp Dijon mustard

1 tsp honey or sugar

1 red pepper, cored, deseeded and chopped

½ yellow pepper, cored, deseeded and chopped

½ green pepper, cored, deseeded and chopped

1 red onion, finely chopped

½ cucumber, peeled, deseeded and chopped (optional)

3 tomatoes, deseeded and chopped

2–3 tbsp chopped flat-leaved parsley

salt and pepper

TO SERVE

12 cherry tomatoes, halved

12 black olives, stoned and chopped

1 tbsp flaked almonds, toasted

1 Heat 2 tablespoons of the oil in a large saucepan. Add the onion and cook for 2 minutes, stirring frequently, until beginning to soften. Stir in half the garlic and cook for a further minute.

2 Add the rice, stirring well to coat, and cook for about 2 minutes until translucent. Stir in the stock and half the thyme and bring to the boil; season with salt and pepper. Simmer very gently, covered, for about 20 minutes until tender. Stand, still covered, for about 15 minutes; uncover and cool completely.

3 Whisk the vinegar with the remaining garlic and thyme, the mustard, honey and salt and pepper in a large bowl. Slowly whisk in about 90 ml/3¼ fl oz of the olive oil. Using a fork, fluff the rice into the vinaigrette.

4 Add the peppers, red onion, cucumber, tomatoes and parsley; toss and season.

5 Transfer to a serving bowl and garnish with the tomatoes, olives and almonds. Serve warm.

Thai-style Caesar Salad

Serves 4

INGREDIENTS

1 large head cos lettuce, with
outer leaves removed,
or 2 hearts
vegetable oil, for deep frying
4–6 large rice paper wrappers or
115 g/4 oz rice paper flakes

small bunch of coriander, leaves
stripped from stems

DRESSING
80 ml/3 fl oz rice vinegar
2–3 tbsp Thai fish sauce
2 garlic cloves, roughly chopped

1 tbsp sugar
2.5 cm/1 inch piece fresh ginger
root, peeled and coarsely
chopped
125 ml/4 fl oz sunflower oil
salt and pepper

1 Tear the lettuce leaves into bite-sized pieces and put into a large salad bowl.

2 To make the dressing, put the vinegar, fish sauce, garlic, sugar and ginger in a food processor and process for 15–30 seconds.

3 With the machine running, gradually pour in the sunflower oil until a creamy liquid forms. Season with salt and pepper and pour into a jug; set aside.

4 Heat about 7.5 cm/ 3 inches of vegetable oil in a deep-fat fryer to 190°C/375°F.

5 Meanwhile, break the rice wrappers into bite-sized pieces and dip each into a bowl of water to soften. Lay on a clean tea towel and pat completely dry.

6 Working in batches, add the rice paper pieces to the hot oil and fry for about 15 seconds until crisp and golden. Using a slotted spoon, transfer to kitchen paper to drain.

7 Add the coriander leaves to the lettuce and toss to mix. Add the fried rice paper 'crisps' and drizzle over the dressing. Toss to coat the leaves and serve immediately.

VARIATION

Substitute 2 tablespoons of the sunflower oil with sesame oil for a different flavour.

Brown Rice, Lentil & Shiitake Salad

Serves 6-8

INGREDIENTS

225 g/8 oz Puy lentils, rinsed
4 tbsp olive oil
1 onion, finely chopped
200 g/7 oz long-grain brown rice
½ tsp dried thyme
450 ml/16 fl oz chicken stock
350 g/12 oz shiitake mushrooms,
    trimmed and sliced
2 garlic cloves, finely chopped

115 g/4 oz smoked bacon, diced
    and fried until crisp
2 small courgettes, diced
1-2 sticks celery, thinly sliced
6 spring onions, thinly sliced
2-3 tbsp chopped fresh
    flat-leaved parsley
2 tbsp walnut halves, toasted and
    roughly chopped
salt and pepper

DRESSING
2 tbsp red or white wine vinegar
1 tbsp balsamic vinegar
1 tsp Dijon mustard
1 tsp sugar
80 ml/3 fl oz extra-virgin olive oil
2-3 tbsp walnut oil

1 Bring a large saucepan of water to the boil. Add the lentils, bring back to the boil, then simmer for about 30 minutes until just tender; do not overcook. Drain and rinse under cold running water; drain and set aside.

2 Heat 2 tablespoons of the oil in a large saucepan. Add the onion and cook until it begins to soften. Add the rice; stir to coat. Add the thyme, stock and salt and pepper; bring to the boil. Simmer very gently, covered tightly, for about 40 minutes until the rice is tender and the liquid absorbed.

3 Heat the remaining oil in a frying pan and stir-fry the mushrooms for about 5 minutes until golden. Stir in the garlic and cook for a further 30 seconds. Season with salt and pepper.

4 To make the dressing, whisk together the vinegars, mustard and sugar in a large bowl. Gradually whisk in the oils. Season with salt and pepper. Add the lentils and gently toss. Fork in the rice. Toss.

5 Stir in the bacon and mushrooms, then the courgettes, celery, spring onions and parsley and season. Serve sprinkled with walnuts.

Moroccan Mixed Rice Salad

Serves 4–6

INGREDIENTS

800 ml/1¹/₃ pints water	1 small red pepper, deseeded and	SPICED DRESSING
1 tbsp soy sauce	diced	1 tsp hot curry powder
1 tbsp unsulphured molasses	85 g/3 oz ready-soaked dried	1 tsp ground coriander
75 g/2³/₄ oz wild rice	apricots, sliced	1 tsp ground turmeric
2 tbsp olive oil	75 g/2³/₄ oz raisins	1 tsp freshly ground nutmeg
100 g/3¹/₂ oz long-grain brown or	2 tbsp chopped fresh mint or	1/2 tsp cayenne pepper
white rice	coriander	50 ml/2 fl oz rice vinegar
425 g/15 oz can chickpeas rinsed	60 g/2¹/₄ oz flaked almonds,	2 tbsp honey
and drained	toasted	1 tbsp lemon juice
¹/₂ red onion, finely chopped	lettuce leaves, to garnish	80 ml/3 fl oz extra-virgin olive oil
	lemon wedges, to serve	

1 Put 350 ml/12 fl oz of the water, the soy sauce and molasses in a saucepan and bring to the boil. Add the wild rice and bring back to the boil. Cover and simmer gently for 30–50 minutes depending on whether you prefer a chewy or tender texture. Remove from the heat to cool slightly.

2 Heat the oil in a saucepan, add the brown rice and stir for about 2 minutes to coat with the oil. Add the remaining water and bring to the boil; reduce the heat to low and simmer, covered tightly, for about 40 minutes until the rice is tender and all the water is absorbed. Remove from the heat to cool slightly.

3 Meanwhile, make the dressing; put the ground spices in a small frying pan and cook gently for 4–5 minutes, stirring, until golden. Cool on a small plate. Whisk together the vinegar, honey and lemon juice in a large bowl, then whisk in the oil, until the dressing thickens. Whisk in the cooled spice mixture.

4 Fork the brown rice and wild rice into the dressing and mix well. Stir in the chickpeas, onion, pepper, apricots, raisins and mint.

5 To serve, sprinkle with the almonds, garnish with lettuce and serve with lemon wedges.

Pesto Risotto-rice Salad

Serves 4–6

INGREDIENTS

3 tbsp extra-virgin olive oil
1 onion, finely chopped
200 g/7 oz arborio rice
450 ml/16 fl oz boiling water
6 sun-dried tomatoes, cut into
    thin slivers
1/2 small red onion, very thinly
    sliced
3 tbsp lemon juice

PESTO
50 g/2 oz lightly packed fresh
    basil leaves
2 garlic cloves, finely chopped
2 tbsp pine kernels, lightly
    toasted
125 ml/4 fl oz extra-virgin
    olive oil

50 g/1¾ oz freshly grated
    Parmesan cheese
salt and pepper

TO GARNISH
fresh basil leaves
Parmesan shavings

1 To make the pesto, put the basil, garlic and pine kernels in a food processor and process for about 30 seconds. With the machine running, gradually pour in the olive oil through the feed tube, until a smooth paste forms. Add the cheese and pulse several times, until blended but still with some texture. Scrape the pesto into a small bowl and season with salt and pepper to taste. Set aside.

2 Heat 1 tablespoon of the oil in a saucepan. Add the onion and cook until beginning to soften. Add the rice and stir to coat. Cook, stirring occasionally, for about 2 minutes. Stir in the boiling water and salt and pepper. Cover and simmer very gently for 20 minutes until the rice is just tender and the water absorbed. Cool slightly.

3 Put the sun-dried tomatoes and sliced onion in a large bowl, add the lemon juice and about 2 tablespoons of oil. Fork in the hot rice and stir in the pesto. Toss to combine. Adjust the seasoning if necessary. Cover and let cool to room temperature.

4 Fork the rice mixture into a shallow serving bowl. Drizzle with some olive oil and garnish with basil leaves and Parmesan. Serve the salad at room temperature, not chilled.

Red Rice Salad with Hot Dressing

Serves 6–8

INGREDIENTS

1 tbsp olive oil
200 g/7 oz red rice
600 ml/1 pint water
400 g/14 oz can red kidney
    beans, rinsed and drained
1 small red pepper, cored,
    deseeded and diced

1 small red onion, finely chopped
2 small cooked beetroots (not in
    vinegar), peeled and diced
6–8 red radishes, thinly sliced
2–3 tbsp chopped fresh chives
salt and pepper
fresh chives, to garnish

HOT DRESSING
2 tbsp prepared horseradish
1 tbsp Dijon mustard
1 tsp sugar
50 ml/2 fl oz red wine vinegar
125 ml/4 fl oz cup extra-virgin
    olive oil

1 Put the olive oil and red rice in a heavy-based saucepan and place over a medium heat. Add the water and 1 teaspoon of salt. Bring to the boil, reduce the heat and simmer, covered, until the rice is tender and all the water is absorbed (see Cook's Tip). Remove from the heat and let the rice cool to room temperature.

2 To make the dressing, put the horseradish, mustard and sugar in a small bowl and whisk to combine. Whisk in the vinegar, then gradually whisk in the oil to form a smooth dressing.

3 In a large bowl, combine the red kidney beans, red pepper, red onion, beetroot, radishes and chives and toss together. Season with salt and pepper.

4 Using a fork, fluff the rice into the bowl with the vegetables and toss together. Pour over the dressing and toss well. Cover and let the salad stand for about 1 hour. Spoon into a large shallow serving bowl, garnish with fresh chives and serve immediately.

COOK'S TIP

There are several red rice varieties on the market. Read the labels carefully as some require longer cooking than others.

Fruity Wild Rice Salsa with Black Beans

Serves 4–6

INGREDIENTS

150 g/5½ oz small black beans, soaked overnight in cold water
1 onion, studded with 4 cloves
150 g/5½ oz wild rice
2 garlic cloves, trimmed
450 ml/16 fl oz boiling water
1 red onion, finely chopped
2 fresh red chillies, deseeded and thinly sliced

1 large red pepper, deseeded and chopped
1 small mango or papaya, peeled and diced
2 oranges, segments removed and juice reserved
4 passion fruits, pulp and juice
juice of 3–4 limes
½ tsp ground cumin

1 tbsp maple syrup or light brown sugar
150 ml/5 fl oz extra-virgin olive oil
1 small bunch coriander, leaves stripped from stems and chopped
lime slices, to garnish

1 Drain the soaked beans and put in a large saucepan with the clove-studded onion. Cover with cold water by at least 5 cm/ 2 inches. Bring to the boil, reduce the heat to low and simmer for 1 hour until the beans are tender. Discard the onion, rinse the beans under cold running water, drain and set aside.

2 Meanwhile, put the wild rice and garlic in a saucepan and cover with the boiling water. Simmer, covered, over a low heat for 30–50 minutes depending on the preferred texture. Cool slightly; discard the garlic cloves.

3 Put the beans in a large bowl and fork in the wild rice. Add the onion, chillies, pepper, mango, orange segments and their juice and the passion fruit pulp and juice. Toss well together.

4 Combine the lime juice, ground cumin and maple syrup. Whisk in the olive oil and half the coriander, then pour over the bean/rice mixture and toss well. Cover and allow the flavours to blend for up to 2 hours.

5 Spoon into a serving bowl, sprinkle with the remaining coriander and serve garnished with lime slices.

Prawn Salad & Toasted Rice

Serves 4

INGREDIENTS

225 g/8 oz raw prawns, with tail shells left on
cayenne pepper
2 tbsp sunflower oil
1 tbsp long-grain white rice
1 large head cos lettuce with outer leaves removed or 2 hearts

½ small English cucumber, lightly peeled, deseeded and thinly sliced
1 small bunch chives, sliced into 2.5 cm/1 inch pieces
handful of fresh mint leaves
salt and pepper

DRESSING
50 ml/2 fl oz rice vinegar
1 red chilli, deseeded and thinly sliced
7.5 cm/3 inch piece lemon grass stalk, crushed
juice of 1 lime
2 tbsp Thai fish sauce
1 tsp sugar, or to taste

1 Split each prawn in half lengthways, leaving the tail attached to one half. Remove any dark intestinal veins and pat dry. Sprinkle with a little salt and cayenne pepper.

2 To make the dressing, combine the vinegar with the chilli and lemon grass. Leave to marinate.

3 Heat the oil in a wok or heavy-based frying pan over high heat. Add the rice and stir until brown and richly fragrant. Turn into a mortar and cool completely. Crush gently with a pestle until coarse crumbs form.

4 Stir-fry the prawns in the cleaned pan for 1 minute until warm. Transfer to a plate and season with pepper.

5 Tear or shred the lettuce into large bite-sized pieces and transfer to a shallow salad bowl. Add the cucumber, chives and mint leaves and toss to combine.

6 Remove the lemon grass and most of the chilli slices from the rice vinegar and whisk in the lime juice, fish sauce and sugar. Pour most of the dressing over the salad and toss. Top with the prawns and drizzle with the remaining dressing. Sprinkle with the toasted rice and serve.

Thai Noodle Salad with Prawns

Serves 4

INGREDIENTS

85 g/3 oz rice vermicelli or rice
    sticks
175 g/6 oz mangetout, cut
    crossways in half, if large
5 tbsp lime juice
4 tbsp Thai fish sauce
1 tbsp sugar, or to taste

2.5 cm/1 inch piece fresh ginger
    root, peeled and finely chopped
1 fresh red chilli, deseeded and
    thinly sliced on the diagonal
4 tbsp chopped fresh coriander or
    mint, plus extra for garnishing
10 cm/4 inch piece of cucumber,
    peeled, deseeded and diced

2 spring onions, thinly sliced on
    the diagonal
16–20 large cooked, peeled
    prawns
2 tbsp chopped unsalted peanuts
    or cashews (optional)
4 whole cooked prawns and
    lemon slices, to garnish

1 Put the rice noodles in a large bowl and pour over enough hot water to cover. Stand for about 4 minutes until soft. Drain and rinse under cold running water; drain and set aside.

2 Bring a saucepan of water to the boil. Add the mangetout (snow peas) and return to the boil. Simmer for 1 minute. Drain, rinse under cold running water until cold, then drain and set aside.

3 In a large bowl, whisk together the lime juice, fish sauce, sugar, ginger, chilli and coriander or mint. Stir in the cucumber and spring onions. Add the drained noodles, mangetout and the prawns. Toss the salad gently together.

4 Divide the noodle salad among 4 large plates. Sprinkle with chopped coriander and the peanuts (if using), then garnish each plate with a whole prawn and a lemon slice. Serve immediately.

COOK'S TIP

There are many sizes of rice noodles available – make sure you use the very thin rice noodles, called rice vermicelli or rice sticks or sen mee, otherwise the salad will be too heavy.

Wild Rice Blini with Smoked Salmon

Makes about 50 blinis

INGREDIENTS

butter or oil for frying
4 spring onions, thinly sliced on
    the diagonal
115 g/4 oz smoked salmon, thinly
    sliced or shredded
125 ml/4 fl oz soured cream
chopped chives, to garnish

BLINIS
80 ml/3 fl oz lukewarm water
1½ tsp dried yeast
60 g/2¼ oz plain flour
70 g/2½ oz buckwheat flour
2 tbsp sugar
½ tsp salt

225 ml/8 fl oz milk
2 eggs, separated
2 tbsp butter, melted
60 g/2¼ oz cooked wild rice

1 Pour the lukewarm water into a small bowl and sprinkle over the yeast. Stand until the yeast has dissolved and the mixture is beginning to bubble.

2 Sift the flours into a large bowl and stir in the sugar and salt. Make a well in the centre. Warm 175 ml/6 fl oz milk and add to the well with the yeast mixture. Gradually whisk the flour into the liquid to form a smooth batter. Cover the bowl with cling film and leave to stand in a warm place until light and bubbly.

3 Beat the remaining milk with the egg yolks and the melted butter and beat into the batter.

4 Using an electric mixer, beat the egg whites until soft peaks form. Fold a spoonful into the batter, then fold in the remaining egg whites and the wild rice alternately; do not over mix.

5 Heat a little butter or oil in a large frying pan to lightly coat. Drop tablespoons of the batter into the pan and cook for 1–2 minutes until tiny bubbles form. Turn and cook for 30 seconds. Remove and keep warm in a low oven while cooking the remaining batter.

6 To serve, top with the spring onions, smoked salmon strips, a dollop of soured cream and a sprinkling of chives.

Main Dishes & Accompaniments

Rice, like wheat, is one of the world's most versatile ingredients. It can be used as the focal point of a main dish or as a subtle accompaniment to roasts and stews.

Use rice as the base of a substantial dish like Chicken Basquaise, to soak up the flavours of South West France, or combine it with lamb and exotic spices to create a delicious Eastern-style pilaf, perfect for informal entertaining. Rice is ideal for making one-pot dishes – Seafood Rice, a marvellous mix of mussels, clams, peppers and chilli, proves the point, or follow the Cuban tradition of serving rice with black beans, sausage and ham for a truly satisfying dish.

Try transforming rice into curried patties, a tasty vegetarian alternative to burgers, or use rice as a foil to the strong flavours of stir-fries – the ginger fried rice dish, topped with succulent soy-glazed duck, is an oriental treat. Noodles made from rice also provide excellent all-in-one dishes – try Pad Thai with chicken and crab for an exotic supper.

Delicate flavours go well with rice, especially if the rice is used as an accompaniment. Lemon-scented Rice with Mint will enhance any dish, from a Middle-Eastern tajine to a French beef casserole, while Fragrant Orange Basmati Rice is the perfect accompaniment to steamed fish or poultry dishes.

Chicken Basquaise

Serves 4–5

INGREDIENTS

1.3 kg/3 lb chicken, cut into
    8 pieces
about 2 tbsp flour, for dusting
2–3 tbsp olive oil
1 large onion, (preferably
    Spanish), thickly sliced
2 peppers, deseeded and cut
    lengthways into thick strips
2 garlic cloves

150 g/5½ oz spicy chorizo
    sausage, peeled, if necessary,
    and cut into 1 cm/
    ½ inch pieces
1 tbsp tomato purée
200 g/7 oz long-grain white rice
    or medium-grain Spanish
    rice, such as valencia
450 ml/16 fl oz chicken stock

1 tsp crushed dried chillies
½ tsp dried thyme
125 g/4½ oz Bayonne or other
    air-dried ham, diced
12 dry-cured black olives
2 tbsp chopped fresh flat-leaved
    parsley
salt and pepper

1 Dry the chicken pieces well with kitchen paper. Put the flour in a polythene bag, season with salt and pepper and add the chicken pieces. Seal the bag and shake to coat the chicken.

2 Heat 2 tablespoons of the oil in a large flameproof casserole over a medium-high heat. Add the chicken and cook for about 15 minutes until well browned. Transfer to a plate.

3 Heat the remaining oil in the pan and add the onion and peppers. Reduce the heat to medium and stir-fry until beginning to colour and soften. Add the garlic, chorizo and tomato purée and continue stirring for about 3 minutes. Add the rice and cook for about 2 minutes, stirring to coat, until the rice is translucent.

4 Add the stock, crushed chillies and thyme and

salt and pepper and stir. Bring to the boil. Return the chicken to the pan, pressing gently into the rice. Cover and cook over a very low heat for about 45 minutes until the chicken and rice are tender.

5 Gently stir the ham, black olives and half the parsley into the rice mixture. Re-cover and heat through for a further 5 minutes. Sprinkle with the remaining parsley and serve.

Pad Thai

Serves 4

INGREDIENTS

225 g/8 oz flat rice noodles (sen lek)

2 tbsp groundnut or vegetable oil

225 g/8 oz boneless chicken breasts, skinned and thinly sliced

4 shallots, finely chopped

2 garlic cloves, finely chopped

4 spring onions, cut on the diagonal into 5 cm/2 inch pieces

350 g/12 oz fresh white crab meat

75 g/2¾ oz fresh beansprouts, rinsed

1 tbsp preserved radish or fresh radish, finely diced

2–4 tbsp roasted peanuts, chopped

fresh coriander sprigs, to garnish

SAUCE

3 tbsp Thai fish sauce

2–3 tbsp rice vinegar or cider vinegar

1 tbsp chilli bean sauce or oyster sauce

1 tbsp toasted sesame oil

1 tbsp palm sugar or light brown sugar

½ tsp cayenne pepper or fresh red chilli, thinly sliced

1 To make the sauce, whisk together the sauce ingredients in a small bowl and set aside.

2 Put the rice noodles in a large bowl and pour over enough hot water to cover; let stand for 15 minutes until softened. Drain, rinse and drain again.

3 Heat the oil in a heavy-based wok over a high heat until very hot, but not smoking. Add the chicken strips and stir-fry for 1–2 minutes until they just begin to colour. Using a slotted spoon, transfer to a plate. Reduce the heat to medium-high.

4 Stir the shallots, garlic and spring onions (scallions) into the wok and stir-fry for about 1 minute. Stir in the drained noodles, then the prepared sauce.

5 Return the reserved chicken to the pan with the crab meat, beansprouts and radish; toss well. Cook for about 5 minutes until heated through, tossing frequently. If the noodles begin to stick, add a little water.

6 Turn into a serving dish and sprinkle with the chopped peanuts. Garnish with coriander and serve immediately.

Stir-fried Ginger Rice with Duck

Serves 4–6

INGREDIENTS

2 duck breasts, cut into thin slices
    on the diagonal
2–3 tbsp Japanese soy sauce
1 tbsp mirin (Japanese sweet
    rice wine) or sherry
2 tsp brown sugar
5 cm/2 inch piece fresh ginger
    root, finely chopped or grated

4 tbsp peanut oil
2 garlic cloves, crushed
300 g/10½ oz long-grain white or
    brown rice
800 ml/1⅓ pints chicken stock
115 g/4 oz cooked lean ham,
    thinly sliced

175 g/6 oz mangetout,
    cut diagonally in half
40 g/1½ oz fresh beansprouts,
    rinsed
8 spring onions, thinly sliced on
    the diagonal
2–3 tbsp chopped fresh coriander
sweet or hot chilli sauce (optional)

1 Put the duck in a shallow bowl with a tablespoon of soy sauce, the mirin, half the brown sugar and one-third of the ginger. Stir to coat; leave to marinate at room temperature.

2 Heat 2–3 tablespoons peanut oil in a large heavy-based saucepan over a medium-high heat. Add the garlic and half the remaining ginger and stir-fry for about 1 minute until fragrant. Add the rice and cook for about 3 minutes, stirring, until translucent and beginning to colour.

3 Add 700 ml/1¼ pints stock and a teaspoon of soy sauce and bring to the boil. Reduce the heat to very low and simmer, covered, for 20 minutes until the rice is tender and the liquid is absorbed. Do not uncover the pan, but remove from the heat and leave to stand.

4 Heat the remaining peanut oil in a large wok. Drain the duck breast and gently stir-fry for about 3 minutes until just coloured. Add 1 tablespoon soy sauce

and the rest of the sugar and cook for 1 minute; remove to a plate and keep warm.

5 Stir in the ham, mangetout, beansprouts, spring onions, the remaining ginger and half the coriander; add about 125 ml/¼ fl oz of the stock and stir-fry for 1 minute, or until the stock is almost reduced. Fork in the rice and toss together. Add a few drops of chilli sauce, to taste.

6 To serve, turn into a serving dish, arrange the duck on top and sprinkle with the remaining coriander.

Azerbaijani Lamb Pilaf

Serves 4–6

INGREDIENTS

2–3 tbsp oil
650 g/1 lb 7 oz boneless lamb
  shoulder, cut into 2.5 cm/
  1 inch cubes
2 onions, coarsely chopped
1 tsp ground cumin
200 g/7 oz arborio, long-grain
  or basmati rice

1 tbsp tomato purée
1 tsp saffron threads
100 ml/3½ fl oz pomegranate
  juice (see Cook's Tip)
850 ml/1½ pints lamb or chicken
  stock, or water
115 g/4 oz dried apricots or
  prunes, ready soaked and
  halved

2 tbsp raisins
salt and pepper

TO SERVE
2 tbsp chopped fresh mint
2 tbsp chopped fresh watercress

1 Heat the oil in a large flameproof casserole or wide saucepan over a high heat. Add the lamb in batches and cook for about 7 minutes, turning, until lightly browned.

2 Add the onions to the casserole, reduce the heat to medium-high and cook for about 2 minutes until beginning to soften. Add the cumin and rice and cook for about 2 minutes, stirring to coat well, until the rice is translucent. Stir in the tomato purée (paste) and the saffron threads.

3 Add the pomegranate juice and stock and bring to the boil, stirring once or twice. Add the apricots or prunes and raisins to the casserole, then stir together. Reduce the heat to low, then cover, and simmer for 20–25 minutes until the lamb and rice are tender and the liquid is absorbed.

4 To serve, sprinkle the chopped mint and watercress over the pilaf and serve from the pan.

COOK'S TIP

Pomegranate juice is available from Middle Eastern grocery stores. If you cannot find it, substitute unsweetened grape or apple juice.

Louisiana 'Dirty' Rice

Serves 6

INGREDIENTS

175 g/6 oz belly pork, diced or thickly sliced bacon
225 g/8 oz chicken livers, trimmed, rinsed, dried and chopped
225 g/8 oz chicken gizzards, trimmed, rinsed, dried and finely chopped

1 onion, finely chopped
1 stick celery, finely chopped
1 green pepper, cored, deseeded and chopped
3–4 garlic cloves, finely chopped
1 tsp ground cumin
1 tsp hot red pepper sauce, or to taste

200 g/7 oz long-grain white rice
600 ml/1 pint chicken stock
2–3 spring onions, sliced
2–3 tbsp chopped fresh flat-leaved parsley
salt and pepper

1 Cook the pork in a large heavy-based saucepan for about 7 minutes until it is crisp and golden. Using a slotted spoon, remove the bacon to a plate. Add the chicken livers and gizzards and cook, stirring occasionally, for about 5 minutes until tender and lightly golden. Transfer to the plate of pork.

2 Add the onion, celery and pepper to the pan and cook for about 6 minutes, stirring frequently, until the vegetables are tender. Stir in the garlic, cumin and hot pepper sauce and cook for a further 30 seconds.

3 Add the rice and cook, stirring, until translucent and well coated with the fat. Add the stock and season with salt and pepper.

4 Return the cooked bacon, chicken livers and gizzards to the pan, stirring to blend. Cover and simmer gently for 20 minutes until the rice is tender and the liquid absorbed.

5 Fork half the spring onions and the parsley into the rice and toss gently together. Transfer to a serving dish, sprinkle with the remaining spring onions and serve immediately.

Moros y Christianos

Serves 8–10

INGREDIENTS

450 g/1 lb dried small black beans, soaked overnight in cold water
1 tbsp vegetable or olive oil
225 g/8 oz belly pork, diced or thickly sliced bacon
1 large onion, chopped (preferably Spanish)
2 ripe tomatoes, deseeded and chopped

2 garlic cloves, finely chopped
1 tsp ground cumin
½ tsp dried crushed chillies
2 fresh bay leaves or 1 dried
1–2 tbsp dark brown sugar
2 litres/3½ pints chicken stock
175 g/6 oz spicy chorizo sausage, peeled if necessary, cut into 1 cm/½ inch slices

900 g/2 lb ham hock
200 g/7 oz long or medium-grain white rice
1–2 tbsp lime juice
1–2 tbsp chopped fresh coriander (optional)
salt and pepper
lime wedges, to garnish

1 Drain the soaked beans and rinse under cold water. Heat the oil in a large flameproof casserole over a medium heat. Add the belly pork or bacon and cook for about 4 minutes until the fat is rendered and the pork is beginning to colour.

2 Add the onion, tomatoes and garlic and cook, stirring frequently, for about 10 minutes until the vegetables are soft. Stir in the cumin, crushed chillies to taste, bay leaves and sugar.

3 Add the drained black beans and stock. Add the chorizo, then the ham hock, pushing it well down. Bring to the boil, skimming off any foam. Partially cover, reduce the heat and simmer gently for about 2 hours, stirring occasionally, until the meat and beans are tender. Remove the ham hock and let cool slightly.

4 Meanwhile, bring a saucepan of water to the boil. Add a pinch of salt and sprinkle in the rice; return to the boil. Reduce the heat and simmer gently for about 20 minutes until the rice is tender. Drain, rinse and set aside.

5 Remove the meat from the ham hock bone, cutting it into pieces, and return it to the beans. Stir in the cooked rice, lime juice and half the coriander. Adjust the seasoning.

6 Transfer to a serving bowl and sprinkle with the remaining coriander. Garnish with the lime wedges and serve hot.

Baked Tomato Rice with Sausages

Serves 4

INGREDIENTS

2 tbsp vegetable oil
1 onion, coarsely chopped
1 red pepper, cored, deseeded
    and chopped
2 garlic cloves, finely chopped
½ tsp dried thyme
300 g/10½ oz long-grain
    white rice

1 litre/1¾ pints light chicken or
    vegetable stock
225 g/8 oz can chopped
    tomatoes
1 bay leaf
2 tbsp shredded fresh basil
175 g/6 oz mature (sharp)
    Cheddar cheese, grated

2 tbsp chopped fresh chives
4 herby pork sausages, cooked
    and cut into 1 cm/
    ½ inch pieces
2–3 tbsp freshly grated Parmesan
    cheese

1 Heat the oil in a large flame-proof casserole over medium heat. Add the onion and red pepper and cook for about 5 minutes, stirring frequently, until soft and lightly coloured. Stir in the garlic and thyme and cook for a further minute.

2 Add the rice and cook, stirring frequently, for about 2 minutes until the rice is well coated and translucent. Stir in the stock, tomatoes and bay leaf. Boil for 5 minutes until the stock is almost absorbed.

3 Stir in the basil, Cheddar cheese, chives and pork sausages and bake, covered, in a preheated oven at 180°C/350°F/Gas Mark 4 for about 25 minutes.

4 Sprinkle with the Parmesan cheese and return to the oven, uncovered, for 5 minutes until the top is golden. Serve hot from the casserole.

VARIATION

For a vegetarian version, replace the pork sausages with a 400 g/14 oz can of drained butter beans, kidney beans, or sweetcorn. Or try a mixture of sautéed mushrooms and courgettes.

Seafood Rice

Serves 4–6

INGREDIENTS

4 tbsp olive oil

16 large raw peeled prawns, tails on if possible

225 g/8 oz cleaned squid or cuttlefish, cut into 1 cm/½ inch slices

2 green peppers, deseeded and cut lengthways into 1 cm/½ inch strips

1 large onion, finely chopped

4 garlic cloves, finely chopped

2 fresh bay leaves or 1 dried

1 tsp saffron threads

½ tsp dried crushed chillies

400 g/14 oz arborio or valencia rice

225 ml/8 fl oz dry white wine

850 ml/1½ pints fish, light chicken or vegetable stock

12–16 littleneck clams, well scrubbed

12–16 large mussels, well scrubbed

salt and pepper

2 tbsp chopped fresh flat-leaved parsley, to garnish

RED PEPPER SAUCE

2–3 tbsp olive oil

2 onions, finely chopped

4–6 garlic cloves, finely chopped

4–6 Italian roasted red peppers in olive oil or roasted, peeled and roughly chopped

425 g/15 oz can chopped tomatoes in juice

1–1½ tsp hot paprika

salt

1 To make the red pepper sauce, heat the oil in a saucepan. Add the onions and cook for 6–8 minutes until golden. Stir in the garlic and cook for a minute. Add the remaining ingredients and simmer gently, stirring occasionally, for about 10 minutes. Process to form a smooth sauce; set aside and keep warm.

2 Heat half the oil in a wide pan over a high heat. Add the prawns and stir-fry for 2 minutes. Transfer to a plate. Add the squid and stir-fry for about 2 minutes until just firm. Add to the prawns.

3 Heat the remaining oil in the pan, add the green peppers and onion and stir-fry for about 6 minutes until just tender. Stir in the garlic, bay leaves, saffron and chillies and cook for 30 seconds. Add the rice and cook, stirring, until well coated.

4 Add the wine and stir until absorbed. Add the stock, salt and pepper. Bring to the boil and cover. Simmer gently for about 20 minutes until the rice is just tender and the liquid is almost absorbed.

5 Add the clams and mussels. Re-cover and cook for about 10 minutes until the shells open. Stir in the prawns and squid. Re-cover and heat through. Sprinkle with parsley; serve with the sauce.

Vietnamese Rice Paper Wraps

Makes 20–30 wraps

INGREDIENTS

225 g/8 oz cooked peeled prawns
225 g/8 oz salmon fillet, seared for
    1 minute each side and cut into
    5 mm/¼ inch slices
225 g/8 oz tuna steak, seared for
    1 minute each side and cut into
    5 mm/¼ inch slices
2 ripe avocados, peeled, sliced and
    sprinkled with lime juice
6–8 asparagus tips, blanched
1 small red onion, thinly sliced
16 spring onions, sliced
12 black Niçoise olives, sliced
14 cherry tomatoes, halved

large bunch of coriander, leaves
    stripped from the stems
20–30 rice paper wrappers,
    preferably 18 cm/7 inch rounds
lime wedges

SPICED VINEGAR DIPPING SAUCE
80 ml/3 fl oz rice vinegar
2 tbsp Thai fish sauce
2 tbsp caster sugar
1 garlic clove, finely chopped
2 red chillies, deseeded and
    thinly sliced
2 tbsp chopped fresh coriander

SOY DIPPING SAUCE
125 ml/4 fl oz Thai fish sauce
4–6 tbsp lime juice
2 tbsp Japanese soy sauce
2–3 tbsp light brown sugar
2.5 cm/1 inch piece fresh ginger
    root, finely chopped
2–4 garlic cloves, minced

1 To make the dipping sauces, put the ingredients for each into separate bowls and stir together to blend.

2 Arrange the prawns, fish, vegetables and coriander leaves on a large serving platter in groups, ready to use as different fillings for the wrappers. Cover loosely with cling film and chill until ready to serve.

3 Dip each wrapper very briefly into a bowl of warm water to soften. Lay on clean tea towels to absorb any excess water, then pile on to a serving plate and cover with a damp tea towel.

4 To serve, let your guests fill their own wrappers. Offer lime wedges for squeezing over the fillings and pass the dipping sauces separately.

Fried Rice Parcels

Serves 4

INGREDIENTS

8 large sheets of rice paper, cut
into 23 cm/9 inch rounds
1 egg white, lightly whisked
sesame seeds, for sprinkling
Soy Dipping Sauce (see page 72),
to serve

FRIED RICE
1–2 tbsp vegetable oil
1 tsp cumin seeds
225 g/8 oz cooked white long-
grain or basmati rice
1 tbsp rice vinegar
1 tbsp soy sauce

1 tsp chilli sauce, or to taste
2 spring onions, finely chopped
115 g/4 oz frozen peas, defrosted
2 tbsp chopped fresh coriander
85 g/3 oz cooked ham or prawns,
diced
salt and pepper

1 Heat the oil in a large heavy-based frying pan. Add the cumin seeds and cook, stirring frequently, for about 1 minute until they begin to pop. Add the rice and stir-fry for 2–3 minutes.

2 Add the vinegar, soy sauce and chilli sauce, and toss with the rice. Add the spring onions, peas, coriander and ham and stir-fry for 2 minutes to heat through. Season with salt and pepper. Remove from the heat and cool slightly.

3 Fill a shallow pan with warm water and quickly draw each sheet of the rice paper through the water to wet lightly. Drain on tea towels.

4 Arrange the rice paper rounds on a work surface and divide the mixture evenly among them. Gather up the edges of the paper and twist to form parcels; tie each loosely with string. Transfer to a lightly oiled baking sheet.

5 Brush the top and sides lightly with the egg white and sprinkle generously with sesame seeds. Bake in a preheated oven at 200°C/400°F/Gas Mark 6 for 15–20 minutes until the rice paper is golden. Serve the parcels hot, with the dipping sauce.

Mexican Tomato Rice with Peas

Serves 6–8

INGREDIENTS

400 g/14 oz long-grain
white rice
1 large onion, chopped
2–3 garlic cloves, peeled and
smashed
350 g/12 oz canned Italian
plum tomatoes
3–4 tbsp olive oil

1 litre/1¾ pints chicken stock
1 tbsp tomato purée
1 Habenero or hot chilli
175 g/6 oz frozen green peas,
defrosted
4 tbsp chopped fresh coriander
salt and pepper

TO SERVE
1 large avocado, peeled, sliced and
sprinkled with lime juice
lime wedges
4 spring onions, chopped
1 tbsp chopped fresh coriander

1 Cover the rice with hot water and leave to stand for 15 minutes. Drain, then rinse under cold running water.

2 Place the onion and garlic in a food processor and process until a smooth purée forms. Scrape into a small bowl and set aside. Put the tomatoes in the food processor and process until smooth, then strain into another bowl, pushing through any solids with a wooden spoon.

3 Heat the oil in a flameproof casserole over a medium heat. Add the rice and cook for 4 minutes, stirring frequently, until golden and translucent. Add the onion purée and cook, stirring frequently, for a further 2 minutes. Add the stock and tomato purée and bring to the boil.

4 Using a pin or long needle, carefully pierce the chilli in 2–3 places. Add to the rice, season with salt and pepper and reduce the heat to low. Simmer, covered, for about 25 minutes until the rice is tender and the liquid just absorbed. Discard the chilli, stir in the peas and coriander and cook for 5 minutes to heat through.

5 To serve, gently fork into a large shallow serving bowl. Arrange the avocado slices and lime wedges on top. Sprinkle the chopped spring onions and coriander over and serve at once.

Fidellos Tostados

Serves 6

INGREDIENTS

350 g/12 oz vermicelli or angel
hair pasta in coils, roughly
broken
100 g/3½ oz long-grain
white rice
3 tbsp extra-virgin olive oil
200 g/7 oz canned chopped
tomatoes, drained

600 ml/1 pint chicken stock or
water, plus extra
if necessary
1 bay leaf
1–2 tsp chopped fresh oregano
or 1 tsp dried oregano
½ tsp dried thyme leaves
salt and pepper

1–2 tbsp sprigs and chopped
fresh oregano or thyme,
to garnish

1 Put the pasta and rice in a dry, large, heavy-based saucepan or flameproof casserole over a medium-high heat and cook for 5–7 minutes, stirring frequently, until light golden. (The pasta will break unevenly, but this does not matter.)

2 Stir in 2 tablespoons of the olive oil, together with the chopped tomatoes, stock, bay leaf, oregano and thyme, then season with about a teaspoon of salt and pepper to taste.

3 Bring to the boil, reduce the heat to medium and simmer for about 8 minutes, stirring frequently, to help unwind and separate the pasta coils.

4 Reduce the heat to low and cook, covered, for about 10 minutes until the rice and pasta are tender and all the liquid absorbed. If the rice and pasta are too firm, add about 120 ml/ 4 fl oz more stock or water and continue to cook, covered, for a further 5 minutes. Remove from the heat.

5 Using a fork, fluff the rice and pasta into a warmed serving bowl and drizzle with the remaining oil. Sprinkle with the herbs; serve immediately.

Red Rice Pilaf with Roasted Root Vegetables

Serves 4–6

INGREDIENTS

125 ml/4 fl oz olive oil

grated rind and juice of 1 orange

2 tbsp balsamic vinegar

2 tsp coriander seeds, lightly crushed

1 bay leaf

$^1/_2$ tsp crushed dried chillies, or to taste

8–10 small raw beetroots, trimmed, scrubbed and halved

250 g/9 oz shallots or baby onions

6–8 baby parsnips, trimmed

4–6 baby carrots, trimmed

1 tsp chopped fresh rosemary leaves

400 g/14 oz red Camargue rice

850 ml/1$^1/_2$ pints hot chicken stock

1 red onion

1 small carrot, cut into matchstick strips

1 leek, cut into 1 cm/$^1/_2$ inch rounds

85 g/3 oz pine kernels, lightly roasted

1 tsp light brown sugar

1–2 tbsp chopped fresh coriander

150 g/5$^1/_2$ oz dried cranberries, sour cherries or raisins, soaked in boiling water for 15 minutes

salt and pepper

TO SERVE

225 ml/8 fl oz soured cream

2 tbsp chopped roasted walnuts

1 Put about 4 tablespoons of the olive oil in a large bowl and whisk in the orange rind and juice, vinegar, coriander seeds, bay leaf and crushed chillies. Add the beetroots, shallots, parsnips and carrots and stir to coat well.

2 Turn into a roasting tin and roast in a preheated oven at 200°C/400°F/Gas Mark 6 for 45–55 minutes until the vegetables are tender, turning occasionally. Remove from the oven, sprinkle with the rosemary and salt and pepper; keep warm.

3 Put the rice in a large saucepan with the hot stock. Place over a medium-high heat and bring to the boil; reduce the heat to low and simmer, covered, for about 40 minutes until the rice is tender and the stock absorbed. Remove from the heat but do not uncover.

4 Heat the remaining oil in a large pan. Add the onion and carrot strips and cook for 8–10 minutes until tender. Add the leek, pine kernels, brown sugar and coriander, and cook for 2–3 minutes until the vegetables are lightly caramelized. Drain the cranberries and stir into the vegetable mixture with the rice. Season with salt and pepper.

5 Arrange the roasted vegetables and rice on a serving platter and top with the soured cream. Sprinkle with the chopped walnuts and serve.

Curried Rice Patties with Tahini Dressing

Serves 4–6

INGREDIENTS

¹/₂ tsp salt

70 g/2¹/₂ oz basmati white or
  brown rice

2 tbsp olive oil

1 red onion, finely chopped

2 garlic cloves

2 tsp curry powder

¹/₂ tsp crushed dried chilli flakes

1 small red pepper, cored, deseeded
  and diced

115 g/4 oz frozen peas, defrosted

1 small leek, finely chopped

1 ripe tomato, skinned, deseeded
  and chopped

310 g/11 oz can chickpeas, drained
  and rinsed

85 g/3 oz fresh white breadcrumbs

1–2 tbsp chopped fresh coriander
  or mint

1 egg, lightly beaten

vegetable oil, for frying

salt and pepper

cucumber slices, to garnish

lime wedges, to serve

DRESSING

125 ml/4 fl oz tahini

2 garlic cloves, gently crushed

¹/₂ tsp ground cumin, or to taste

pinch of cayenne pepper

5 tbsp lemon juice

drizzle of extra-virgin olive oil

about 125 ml/4 fl oz water

1 To make the dressing, blend the tahini, garlic, cumin, cayenne and lemon juice in a food processor until creamy. Slowly pour in the oil, then gradually add the water to make a creamy dressing.

2 Bring a saucepan of water to the boil. Add the salt and sprinkle in the rice; simmer for 15–20 minutes until the rice is just tender. Drain, rinse and set aside.

3 Heat the olive oil in a large pan. Add the onion and garlic and cook until beginning to soften. Stir in the curry powder and chilli and cook for 2 minutes. Add the pepper, peas, leek and tomato and cook gently for 7 minutes until tender. Set aside.

4 Process the chickpeas in the food processor until smooth. Add half the vegetables and process again. Transfer to a large bowl and add the remaining vegetable mixture, breadcrumbs, coriander and egg; mix well. Stir in the rice and season well. Chill for 1 hour, then shape into 4–6 patties.

5 Fry the patties in oil for 6–8 minutes until golden. Garnish with cucumber slices and serve with the dressing and lime wedges.

Spicy Potato-rice Pilaf

Serves 4–6

INGREDIENTS

200 g/7 oz basmati rice, soaked
    in cold water for 20 minutes
2 tbsp vegetable oil
½–¾ tsp cumin seeds
225 g/8 oz potatoes, cut into
    1 cm/½ inch pieces

225 g/8 oz frozen peas, defrosted
1 green chilli, deseeded and
    thinly sliced (optional)
½ tsp salt
1 tsp garam masala
½ tsp ground turmeric

¼ tsp cayenne pepper
600 ml/1 pint water
2 tbsp chopped fresh coriander
1 red onion, finely chopped
natural yogurt, to serve

1 Rinse the soaked rice under cold running water until the water runs clear, drain and set aside.

2 Heat the oil in a large heavy-based saucepan over a medium-high heat. Add the cumin seeds and stir for about 10 seconds until the seeds jump and colour.

3 Add the potatoes, peas and chilli, if using, and stir-fry for about 3 minutes until the potatoes are just beginning to soften.

4 Add the rice and cook, stirring frequently, until well coated and beginning to turn translucent. Stir in the salt, garam masala, turmeric and cayenne pepper, then add the water. Bring to the boil, stirring once or twice, then reduce the heat to medium and simmer, covered, until most of the water is absorbed and the surface is filled with little steam-holes. Do not stir.

5 Reduce the heat to very low and, if possible, raise the pan about 2.5 cm/1 inch above the heat source by resting on a ring. Cover and steam for about 10 minutes longer. Remove from the heat, uncover and put a clean tea towel or paper towels over the rice; re-cover. Stand for 5 minutes.

6 Gently fork the rice and potato mixture into a warmed serving bowl and sprinkle with the coriander and chopped red onion. Serve hot with yogurt handed separately.

Turkish Carrot Pilaf

Serves 6

INGREDIENTS

4 tbsp butter
2 carrots, coarsely grated
½ tsp whole black peppercorns
pinch of salt

4–6 ready-soaked dried apricots,
   thinly sliced (optional)
1 tsp sugar
400 g/14 oz long-grain white rice

700 ml/1¼ pints chicken stock
1–2 tbsp chopped green
   pistachios, for sprinkling
   (optional)

1 Melt the butter in a large, heavy-based saucepan over a medium heat. Add the grated carrots and whole peppercorns with a pinch of salt and cook, stirring frequently, for about 3 minutes until the carrots begin to soften.

2 Add the apricots, if using, and sprinkle with the sugar, stirring to combine. Stir in the rice and cook, stirring frequently, for about 3 minutes until the rice is coated with butter and is translucent.

3 Pour in the stock and bring to the boil. Reduce the heat to low and simmer, covered, for 20–25 minutes until the rice is tender and the stock is completely absorbed. Remove from the heat and uncover. Place a folded tea towel or kitchen paper over the rice and re-cover. Stand for about 10 minutes for any steam to be absorbed.

4 Fork the rice into a shallow serving bowl and shape into a rounded dome; sprinkle with the pistachios, if using, and serve hot.

COOK'S TIP

As an alternative serving idea, spoon the pilaf into an oiled ring mould, pressing lightly to compress the rice. Cover the mould with an up-turned serving plate and, holding the plate and mould firmly together, invert quickly, giving a good shake. Gently remove the mould. Fill the centre with chopped pistachios and garnish with a sprig of parsley and cooked carrot strips.

Coconut-scented Brown Rice

Serves 4–6

INGREDIENTS

350 ml/12 fl oz water
225 ml/8 fl oz coconut milk
1 tsp salt
200 g/7 oz long-grain brown rice
1 lemon

1 cinnamon stick
about 15 whole cloves
1 tbsp chopped fresh parsley
fresh coconut shavings (optional)

1 Bring the water to the boil in a heavy-based saucepan and whisk in the coconut milk. Return the liquid to the boil, add the salt and sprinkle in the rice.

2 Pare 2–3 strips of lemon rind and add to the saucepan with the cinnamon stick and the cloves.

3 Reduce the heat to low, cover, and simmer gently for about 45 minutes until the rice is tender and the liquid is completely absorbed. Uncover and leave the rice over high heat for about 1 minute, to let any steam escape and the rice dry out a little bit.

4 Remove the cloves, if wished, then sprinkle with the herbs and coconut, if using; fork into a warmed serving bowl and serve.

COOK'S TIP

This technique can be used to cook white rice as well, but the fuller flavour of brown rice works well with the warm flavour of the spices.

VARIATIONS

The whole cloves can be replaced with a pinch of ground allspice.

•

For a more South-East Asian flavour, use 1 red chilli, pierced in 2–3 places with a pin, a bruised lime leaf and a 7.5 cm/3 inch piece of lemon grass, lightly crushed, instead of the lemon and cloves.

Fragrant Orange Basmati Rice

Serves 4–6

INGREDIENTS

1–2 tbsp butter
3–4 shallots, finely chopped
200 g/7 oz basmati rice
2.5 cm/1 inch piece of fresh
    ginger root, peeled

1–2 fresh bay leaves, lightly
    bruised
2 star anise
1 small cinnamon stick
grated rind and juice of 1 orange
1 tbsp raisins, finely chopped

300 ml/10 fl oz light chicken
    stock or water
salt and pepper
fresh coriander leaves, to garnish
    (optional)

1 Melt the butter in a heavy-based saucepan placed over a medium heat. Add the shallots and cook for 2–3 minutes until beginning to soften.

2 Add the rice and cook, stirring frequently, for 3 minutes until the rice is well coated with the butter and is translucent. Using a large heavy knife, crush the piece of ginger lightly. Add to the pan with the bay leaves, star anise and cinnamon stick. Add the grated rind and orange juice and the raisins and stir.

3 Add the stock and bring to the boil. Season with salt and pepper and reduce the heat. Cover and cook over a low heat for 15–18 minutes until the rice is tender and the liquid completely absorbed.

Remove from the heat, uncover and place a clean tea towel over the rice. Re-cover and stand for up to 20 minutes.

4 Fork the rice into a serving bowl and remove the bay leaves, star anise and cinnamon stick (or keep them in for decoration). Sprinkle the top with a few coriander leaves, if wished, and serve hot.

Lemon-scented Rice with Mint

Serves 4

INGREDIENTS

2 tbsp olive oil or butter
2–4 spring onions,
    finely chopped
3–4 tbsp chopped fresh mint
300 g/10½ oz long-grain
    white rice

500 ml/18 fl oz chicken stock,
    preferably homemade
1 lemon
salt and pepper

TO GARNISH
2–3 mint sprigs
thin lemon and lime slices

1 Heat the oil or butter in a medium heavy-based saucepan over a medium-high heat. Add the spring onions and mint and cook, stirring, for about 1 minute until brightly coloured and fragrant.

2 Add the rice and cook, stirring frequently, for about 2 minutes until well coated with the oil or butter and just translucent. Add the chicken stock and bring to the boil, stirring once or twice. Season with salt and pepper to taste.

3 Pare 3–4 strips of lemon rind and add to the pan; squeeze the juice from the lemon and stir into the rice and stock.

4 When the stock comes to the boil, reduce the heat to low and simmer gently, tightly covered, for about 20 minutes until the rice is tender and the stock absorbed. Remove the pan from the heat and stand for 5–10 minutes.

5 Fork the rice into a serving bowl, garnish with mint and lemon and lime slices. Serve hot.

COOK'S TIP

This basic technique for pilaf rice can be used with other flavour combinations and herbs. The important thing is to fry the rice until well coated and add just enough water to be absorbed by the rice.

Fruity Rice Stuffing

Serves 4

INGREDIENTS

4 fresh poussins
4–6 tbsp butter, melted

STUFFING
225 ml/8 fl oz port
125 g/4½ oz raisins
115 g/4 oz dried no-soak
    apricots, sliced
2–3 tbsp extra-virgin olive oil

1 onion, finely chopped
1 stalk celery, thinly sliced
2 garlic cloves, finely chopped
1 tsp ground cinnamon
1 tsp dried oregano
1 tsp dried mint or basil
½ tsp allspice or ¼ tsp cloves
225 g/8 oz unsweetened chestnuts,
    canned or vacuum-packed

200 g/7 oz long-grain white rice,
    cooked
grated rind and juice of 2 oranges
350 ml/12 fl oz chicken stock
50 g/13/4 oz walnut halves, lightly
    toasted and chopped
2 tbsp chopped fresh mint
2 tbsp chopped fresh flat-leaved
    parsleysalt and pepper

1 To make the stuffing, combine the port, raisins and apricots in a small bowl and let stand for about 15 minutes.

2 Heat the oil in a large heavy-based saucepan. Add the onion and celery and cook for 3–4 minutes. Add the garlic, all the spices and the chestnuts and cook for about 4 minutes, stirring occasionally. Add the rice and half the orange rind and juice, then pour in the stock.

Simmer gently for 5 minutes until most of the liquid is absorbed.

3 Drain the raisins and apricots, reserving the port, and stir into the rice mixture with the walnuts, mint and parsley; cook for a further 2 minutes. Season with salt and pepper, then remove from the heat and cool.

4 Rub the poussins inside and out with salt and

pepper. Lightly fill the cavity of each bird with the stuffing; do not pack too tightly. Tie the legs of each bird together, tucking in the tail. Form extra stuffing into balls.

5 Arrange the birds in a roasting tin with any stuffing balls and brush with melted butter. Drizzle any remaining butter around the pan. Pour over the remaining orange rind and juice and the reserved port.

6 Roast in a preheated oven at 180°C/350°F/ Gas Mark 4 for about 45 minutes, basting, until cooked. Transfer to a platter, cover with foil and rest for 5 minutes. Serve with any pan juices.

Mixed Rice Stuffing with Wild Mushrooms

Makes enough to stuff 1 large chicken or small turkey

INGREDIENTS

4 tbsp butter or oil
6 shallots, finely chopped
175 g/6 oz wild rice
600 ml/1 pint chicken stock
1 bay leaf
½ tsp dried thyme or 2–3 sprigs fresh

200 g/7 oz long-grain white rice
60 g/2¼ oz dried wild mushrooms
225 g/8 oz fresh mushrooms, sliced
2 garlic cloves, finely chopped
3–4 tbsp Madeira wine

85 g/3 oz pecan or walnut halves,
    toasted and roughly chopped
3–4 tbsp chopped fresh flat-leaved
    parsley
2 tbsp chopped fresh chives
salt and pepper

1 Heat half the butter or oil in a large saucepan. Add half the shallots and cook until beginning to soften. Stir in the wild rice to coat, then add 350 ml/ 12 fl oz of the chicken stock, the bay leaf and thyme and bring to the boil. Simmer gently, covered, for about 20 minutes until the stock is absorbed. The wild rice will not be completely cooked.

2 Add the white rice and the remaining stock and season with salt and pepper. Bring to the boil again,

stirring once or twice, then simmer gently, covered, for 20–25 minutes until the stock is absorbed and all the rice is tender. Remove from the heat and stand, covered, for 10–15 minutes.

3 Meanwhile, cover the wild mushrooms with boiling water and leave to soften for about 30 minutes. Lift the mushrooms out and pat dry. Slice thinly.

4 Heat the remaining butter or oil in a large frying pan. Add the

remaining shallots and cook for 3 minutes. Add the mushrooms, garlic and Madeira and stir-fry for 3–4 minutes until golden, stirring occasionally, until all the liquid is absorbed. Turn into a large bowl.

5 Using a fork, fluff the rice into the bowl with the mushrooms, add the chopped nuts, parsley and chives and adjust the seasoning; toss together. Cool before using as a stuffing.

Risottos

One of the great gastronomic feats of Italian cooking, risotto is made with a special rice to create a deliciously creamy dish. It is surprisingly simple to make, but does require a little patience because it involves slow cooking and constant stirring. As long as you use the correct rice and a good homemade stock, and take your time, you'll be on your way to making a perfect risotto!

The recipes in this chapter illustrate the versatility of risotto. Here you'll find something for every occasion – Easy Cheesy Risotto with Parmesan shows you the basic, easy-to-make method, risotto with asparagus or wild mushrooms is guaranteed to give a mid-week meal a lift, while glamorous Champagne Risotto and interesting Black Risotto or Fennel Risotto with Vodka make memorable dinner party dishes. Risotto flavoured with sun-dried tomatoes and Italian cheese, or Minted Risotto with Herbs makes perfect food for family gatherings.

As a change from the classic risotto, try scrumptious Cheese-topped Risotto Tart with Spinach or little Arrancini, irresistible fried risotto balls. There's even a tasty oven-baked risotto, with pancetta and mushrooms.

Easy Cheesy Risotto with Parmesan

Serves 4–6

INGREDIENTS

4–5 tbsp unsalted butter
1 onion, finely chopped
300 g/10½ oz arborio or
    carnaroli rice

125 ml/4 fl oz dry white
    vermouth or white wine
1.2 litres/2 pints chicken or
    vegetable stock, simmering

85 g/3 oz freshly grated
    Parmesan cheese, plus extra
    for sprinkling
salt and pepper

1 Heat about 2 tbsp of the butter in a large heavy-based saucepan over a medium heat. Add the onion and cook for about 2 minutes until just beginning to soften. Add the rice and cook for about 2 minutes, stirring frequently, until translucent and well coated with the butter.

2 Pour in the vermouth: it will bubble and steam rapidly and evaporate almost immediately. Add a ladleful (about 225 ml/8 fl oz) of the simmering stock and cook, stirring constantly, until the stock is absorbed.

3 Continue adding the stock, about half a ladleful at a time, letting each addition be absorbed before adding the next – never let the rice cook 'dry'. This should take 20–25 minutes. The risotto should have a creamy consistency and the rice grains should be tender, but still firm to the bite.

4 Remove the pan from the heat and stir in the remaining butter and Parmesan. Season with salt and a little pepper, to taste. Cover, stand for about 1 minute, then serve immediately with extra Parmesan for sprinkling.

COOK'S TIP

If you prefer not to use butter, soften the onion in 2 tablespoons olive oil and stir in about 2 tablespoons extra-virgin olive oil with the Parmesan at the end.

Risotto with Asparagus

Serves 6

INGREDIENTS

900 g/2 lb fresh asparagus, washed
2 tbsp sunflower or other vegetable oil
6 tbsp unsalted butter

2 shallots or 1 small onion, finely chopped
400 g/14 oz arborio or carnaroli rice
1.5 litres/2¾ pints light chicken or vegetable stock, simmering

85 g/3 oz freshly grated Parmesan cheese
salt and pepper
Parmesan shavings, to garnish (optional)

1 Lightly peel the stems of the asparagus; trim off the woody ends. Cut the tips off each stalk and set aside. Cut the remaining stems into 2.5 cm/1 inch pieces.

2 Add the asparagus stem pieces to a pan of boiling water and boil for 2 minutes. Add the asparagus tips and boil for about 1 minute until tender-crisp; do not overcook. Rinse under cold running water and set aside.

3 Heat the oil with half the butter in a large heavy-based saucepan. Add the shallots and cook gently for about 2 minutes until softened. Add the rice and cook, stirring frequently, for about 2 minutes until the rice is translucent and well coated.

4 Add a ladleful (about 225 ml/8 fl oz) of the simmering stock; it will bubble and steam rapidly. Cook, stirring constantly, until the stock is completely absorbed.

5 Continue adding the stock, about half a ladleful at a time, letting each addition be absorbed before adding the next – never let the rice cook 'dry'. This should take 20–25 minutes. The risotto should have a creamy consistency and the rice should be tender, but firm to the bite.

6 Heat the asparagus tips in the stock. Stir the stems into the risotto with the last ladleful of stock, the remaining butter and Parmesan. Remove from the heat and stir in the asparagus tips and season if necessary. Serve with Parmesan shavings, if wished.

Lemon Risotto with Peas & Mint

Serves 4–6

INGREDIENTS

1.5 litres/2¾ pints chicken stock	300 g/10½ oz arborio or carnaroli rice	60 g/2¼ oz freshly grated Parmesan cheese
4–5 fresh mint sprigs	grated rind and juice of 1 large unwaxed lemon	salt and pepper
2 tbsp extra-virgin olive oil		lemon wedges, to garnish
6 tbsp unsalted butter	175 g/6 oz fresh shelled peas, lightly cooked	
2–3 large shallots, finely chopped		

1 Bring the stock to the boil in a large saucepan. Strip the leaves from the mint sprigs and set aside; gently 'bruise' the mint stems and add to the stock. Reduce the heat and keep the stock at a gentle simmer.

2 Heat the oil and half the butter in a large heavy-based saucepan over medium heat. Add the shallots and cook for about 2 minutes until soft. Add the rice and cook, stirring frequently, for about 2 minutes until the rice is translucent and well coated.

3 Leaving aside the mint stems, add a ladleful (about 225 ml/8 fl oz) of the simmering stock; it will steam and bubble rapidly. Cook, stirring constantly until the stock is absorbed.

4 Continue adding the stock, about half a ladleful at a time, letting each addition be absorbed before adding the next. This should take 20–25 minutes. The risotto should have a creamy consistency and the rice should be tender but firm to the bite.

5 Stir in the lemon rind and juice and the peas; cook until heated through, adding a little more stock or water if the risotto becomes too thick. Remove the pan from the heat and stir in the Parmesan and remaining butter. Season to taste with salt and pepper.

6 Chop the reserved mint leaves and stir into the risotto. Serve immediately with lemon wedges.

Minted Green Risotto with Herbs

Serves 6

INGREDIENTS

2 tbsp unsalted butter

450 g/1 lb fresh shelled peas, or
defrosted frozen peas

1 kg/2 lb 4 oz fresh young spinach
leaves, washed and drained

1 bunch fresh mint, leaves stripped
from stalks

2 tbsp chopped fresh basil

2 tbsp chopped fresh oregano

large pinch of freshly grated nutmeg

4 tbsp mascarpone or double cream

2 tbsp vegetable oil

1 onion, finely chopped

4 sticks celery, including leaves,
finely chopped

2 garlic cloves, finely chopped

½ tsp dried thyme

300 g/10½ oz arborio or
carnaroli rice

50 ml/2 fl oz dry white vermouth

1 litre/1¾ pints light chicken or
vegetable stock, simmering

85 g/3 oz freshly grated
Parmesan cheese

1 Heat half the butter in a deep frying pan over a medium-high heat until sizzling. Add the peas, spinach, mint leaves, basil and oregano; season with the nutmeg. Cook for about 3 minutes, stirring frequently, until the spinach and mint leaves are wilted. Cool slightly.

2 Pour the spinach mixture into a food processor and process for 15 seconds. Add the mascarpone and process again for about 1 minute. Transfer to a bowl and set aside.

3 Heat the oil and remaining butter in a large, heavy-based saucepan over a medium heat. Add the onion, celery, garlic and thyme and cook for about 2 minutes until the vegetables are softened. Add the rice and cook, stirring frequently, for about 2 minutes until the rice is translucent and well coated.

4 Add the vermouth to the rice; it will bubble and steam rapidly. When it is almost absorbed, add a ladleful (about 225 ml/ 8 fl oz) of the simmering stock. Cook, stirring constantly, until the stock is completely absorbed.

5 Continue adding the stock, about half a ladleful at a time, letting each addition be absorbed before adding the next. This should take 20–25 minutes. The risotto should have a creamy consistency and the rice should be just tender. Stir in the spinach-cream mixture and the Parmesan. Serve immediately.

Fennel Risotto with Vodka

Serves 4–6

INGREDIENTS

2 large fennel bulbs
2 tbsp vegetable oil
6 tbsp unsalted butter
1 large onion, finely chopped
350 g/12 oz arborio or
    carnaroli rice

150 ml/5 fl oz vodka (or lemon-
    flavoured vodka, if you can
    find it)
1.3 litres/2¼ pints light chicken
    or vegetable stock, simmering

60 g/2¼ oz freshly grated
    Parmesan cheese
5–6 tbsp lemon juice
salt and pepper

1 Trim the fennel, reserving the fronds for the garnish, if wished. Cut the bulbs in half lengthways and remove the V-shaped cores; roughly chop the flesh. (If you like, add any of the fennel trimmings to the stock for extra flavour.)

2 Heat the oil and half the butter in a large heavy-based saucepan over a medium heat. Add the onion and fennel and cook for about 2 minutes, stirring frequently, until the vegetables are softened.

Add the rice and cook for about 2 minutes, stirring frequently, until the rice is translucent and well coated.

3 Pour in the vodka; it will bubble rapidly and evaporate almost immediately. Add a ladleful (about 225 ml/8 fl oz) of the stock. Cook, stirring constantly, until the stock is absorbed.

4 Continue adding the stock, about half a ladleful at a time, letting each addition be absorbed before adding the next – never let

the rice cook 'dry'. This should take 20–25 minutes. The risotto should have a creamy consistency and the rice should be tender, but firm to the bite.

5 Stir in the remaining butter, with the Parmesan and lemon juice. Remove from the heat, cover and stand for 1 minute. Serve immediately, garnished with a few of the fennel fronds, if wished.

Risotto with Cannellini Beans

Serves 6–8

INGREDIENTS

300 g/10½ oz cannellini beans, soaked and cooked according to packet instructions

2–3 tbsp olive oil

1 large red (or sweet white) onion, finely chopped

3–4 sticks celery, finely chopped

115 g/4 oz pancetta or thick-cut smoky bacon

2–3 garlic cloves, minced

¾ tsp dried oregano or 1 tbsp chopped fresh oregano

400 g/14 oz arborio or carnaroli rice

1 litre/1¾ pints chicken stock, simmering

4 tbsp unsalted butter at room temperature

115 g/4 oz freshly grated Parmesan cheese

salt and pepper

1 Mash, or press through a food mill, half of the cannellini beans and set aside.

2 Heat the olive oil in a large heavy-based saucepan over a medium heat. Add the onion and celery and cook for about 2 minutes until softened. Add the pancetta, garlic and oregano and cook for a further 1–2 minutes, stirring occasionally. Add the rice and cook, stirring frequently, for about 2 minutes until it is translucent and well coated with the oil.

3 Add a ladleful (about 225 ml/ 8 fl oz) of the simmering stock; it will bubble and steam rapidly. Cook, stirring constantly, until the stock is absorbed.

4 Continue adding the stock, about half a ladleful at a time, letting each addition be absorbed before adding the next. This should take 20–25 minutes. The risotto should have a creamy consistency and the rice should be tender, but still firm to the bite.

5 Stir in the beans and the bean purée, season with salt and pepper and heat through. Add a little more stock if necessary.

6 Remove from the heat and stir in the butter and half the Parmesan. Cover and stand for about 1 minute. Serve with the remaining Parmesan sprinkled over.

Champagne Risotto

Serves 4–6

INGREDIENTS

2 tbsp vegetable oil
115 g/4 oz unsalted butter
2 shallots, finely chopped
300 g/10½ oz arborio or
    carnaroli rice

about 600 ml/1 pint Champagne
    or dry sparkling white wine
700 ml/1¼ pints light chicken
    stock, simmering

60 g/2¼ oz freshly grated
    Parmesan cheese
salt and pepper
4–6 large cooked prawns, to
    garnish (optional)

1 Heat the oil and half the butter in a large heavy-based saucepan over a medium heat. Add the shallots and cook for about 2 minutes, until softened. Add the rice and cook, stirring frequently, for about 2 minutes until the rice is translucent and well coated (see Cook's Tip).

2 Pour in half the Champagne; it will bubble and steam rapidly. Cook, stirring constantly, until the liquid is absorbed. Add a ladleful (about 225 ml/8 fl oz) of the simmering stock to the pan and cook, stirring constantly, until the liquid is absorbed.

3 Continue adding the stock, about half a ladleful at a time, letting each addition be absorbed before adding the next – never let the rice cook 'dry'. This should take 20–25 minutes. The risotto should have a creamy consistency and the rice should be tender, but firm to the bite.

4 Stir in the remaining champagne and cook for a further 2–3 minutes.

Remove from the heat and stir in the remaining butter and Parmesan. Season with salt and pepper to taste.

5 Spoon the risotto into serving bowls and garnish each portion with a prawn, if wished. Serve immediately.

COOK'S TIP

It is important to heat and coat the rice at this stage as it will help give the rice its creamy texture.

Wild Mushroom Risotto

Serves 6

INGREDIENTS

60 g/2¼ oz dried porcini or morel
    mushrooms
about 500 g/1 lb 2 oz mixed fresh
    wild mushrooms, such as
    porcini, girolles, horse
    mushrooms and chanterelles,
    cleaned and halved if large

4 tbsp olive oil
3–4 garlic cloves, finely chopped
4 tbsp unsalted butter
1 onion, finely chopped
350 g/12 oz arborio or carnaroli rice
50 ml/2 fl oz dry white vermouth

1.2 litres/2 pints chicken stock,
    simmering
115 g/4 oz freshly grated
    Parmesan cheese
4 tbsp chopped fresh flat-leaved
    parsley
salt and pepper

1 Cover the dried mushrooms with boiling water. Leave to soak for 30 minutes, then carefully lift out and pat dry. Strain the soaking liquid through a sieve lined with kitchen paper, and set aside.

2 Trim the wild mushrooms and gently brush clean.

3 Heat 3 tablespoons of the oil in a large frying pan until hot. Add the fresh mushrooms, and stir-fry for 1–2 minutes. Add the garlic

and the soaked mushrooms and cook for 2 minutes, stirring frequently. Scrape on to a plate and set aside.

4 Heat the remaining oil and half the butter in a large heavy-based saucepan. Add the onion and cook for about 2 minutes until softened. Add the rice and cook, stirring frequently, for about 2 minutes until translucent and well coated.

5 Add the vermouth to the rice. When almost absorbed, add a ladleful

(about 225 ml/8 fl oz) of the simmering stock. Cook, stirring constantly, until the liquid is absorbed.

6 Continue adding the stock, about half a ladleful at a time, letting each addition be absorbed before adding the next. This should take 20–25 minutes. The risotto should have a creamy consistency and the rice should be tender, but firm to the bite.

7 Add half the dried mushroom soaking liquid to the risotto and stir in the mushrooms. Season with salt and pepper, and add more mushroom liquid if necessary. Remove from the heat; stir in the remaining butter, Parmesan and parsley. Serve immediately.

Risotto Primavera

Serves 6–8

INGREDIENTS

225 g/8 oz fresh thin asparagus
    spears, well rinsed
4 tbsp olive oil
175 g/6 oz young green beans, cut
    into 2.5 cm/1 inch pieces
175 g/6 oz young courgettes,
    quartered and cut into 2.5 cm/
    1 inch lengths

225 g/8 oz fresh shelled peas
1 onion, finely chopped
1–2 garlic cloves, finely chopped
350 g/12 oz arborio or carnaroli rice
1.5 litres/2¾ pints chicken stock,
    simmering, plus extra 2 tbsp
4 spring onions, cut into 2.5 cm/
    1 inch lengths

4 tbsp unsalted butter
115 g/4 oz freshly grated Parmesan
    cheese
2 tbsp chopped fresh chives
2 tbsp fresh shredded basil
salt and pepper

1 Trim the woody ends of the asparagus and cut off the tips. Cut the stems into 2.5 cm/ 1 inch pieces and set aside with the tips.

2 Heat 2 tablespoons of the olive oil in a large frying pan over a high heat, until very hot. Add the asparagus, beans, courgettes and peas and stir-fry for 3–4 minutes until they are bright green and just beginning to soften. Set aside.

3 Heat the remaining olive oil in a large heavy-based saucepan over a medium heat. Add the onion and cook for about 1 minute until it begins to soften. Stir in the garlic and cook for 30 seconds. Add the rice and cook, stirring frequently, for 2 minutes until translucent and coated with oil.

4 Add a ladleful (about 225 ml/ 8 fl oz) of the hot stock; the stock will bubble rapidly. Cook, stirring

constantly, until the stock is absorbed.

5 Continue adding the stock, about half a ladleful at a time, letting each addition be absorbed before adding the next – never let the rice cook 'dry'. This should take 20–25 minutes. The risotto should have a creamy consistency and the rice should be tender, but firm to the bite.

6 Stir in the stir-fried vegetables and spring onions with a little more stock. Cook for 2 minutes, stirring frequently, then season. Stir in the butter, Parmesan, chives and basil. Remove from the heat, cover and stand for about 1 minute. Garnish with spring onions, if wished. Serve immediately.

Roasted Pumpkin Risotto

Serves 6

INGREDIENTS

4 tbsp olive oil

4 tbsp unsalted butter, cut into
small pieces

450 g/1 lb pumpkin flesh, cut
into 1 cm/½ inch dice

¾ tsp rubbed sage

2 garlic cloves, finely chopped

2 tbsp lemon juice

2 large shallots, finely chopped

350 g/12 oz arborio or
carnaroli rice

50 ml/2 fl oz dry white vermouth

1.2 litres/2 pints chicken stock,
simmering

60 g/2¼ oz freshly grated
Parmesan cheese

300 g/10½ oz dolcelatte, cut into
small pieces

salt and pepper

celery leaves, to garnish

1 Put half the olive oil and about 1 tbsp of the butter in a roasting tin (pan) and heat in a preheated oven at 200°C/400°F/Gas Mark 6.

2 Add the pumpkin to the pan and sprinkle with the sage, half the garlic and salt and pepper. Toss together and roast for about 10 minutes until just softened and beginning to caramelize. Transfer to a plate.

3 Roughly mash about half the cooked pumpkin

with the lemon juice and reserve with the remaining diced pumpkin.

4 Heat the remaining oil and 1 tbsp of the butter in a large, heavy-based saucepan over a medium heat. Stir in the shallots and remaining garlic and cook for about 1 minute. Add the rice and cook, stirring, for about 2 minutes until well coated.

5 Pour in the vermouth; it will bubble and steam

rapidly. Add a ladleful (about 225 ml/8 fl oz) of the simmering stock and cook, stirring constantly, until the stock is absorbed.

6 Continue adding the stock, about half a ladleful at a time, letting each addition be absorbed before adding the next – never let the rice cook 'dry'. This should take 20–25 minutes. The risotto should have a creamy consistency and the rice should be tender, but firm to the bite.

7 Stir all the pumpkin into the risotto with the remaining butter and the Parmesan. Remove from the heat and fold in the diced dolcelatte. Serve at once, garnished with celery leaves.

Truffle Risotto

Serves 6

INGREDIENTS

2 leeks

115 g/4 oz unsalted butter

300 g/10½ oz arborio or
carnaroli rice

1.2 litres/2 pints chicken stock,
simmering

50 ml/2 fl oz dry white vermouth
or white wine

125 ml/4 fl oz double cream

freshly grated nutmeg

115 g/4 oz freshly grated
Parmesan cheese

115–175 g/4–6 oz fresh black
truffles, brushed clean

50–80 ml/2–3 fl oz truffle oil
(optional)

salt and ¼–½ tsp ground white
pepper

1 Slice the leeks in half lengthways, then shred thinly.

2 Heat half the butter in a large heavy-based pan over medium heat. Add the leeks and cook for about 1 minute until just starting to soften. Add the rice and cook, stirring, until translucent and well coated in butter.

3 Add a ladleful (about 225 ml/8 fl oz) of the hot stock; it will bubble and steam rapidly. Cook, stirring, until the stock is absorbed.

4 Continue adding the stock, about half a ladleful at a time, letting each addition be absorbed before adding the next. This should take 20–25 minutes. The risotto should have a creamy consistency and the rice should be tender, but firm to the bite.

5 Just before the rice is cooked, stir in the vermouth and cream. Season with a little nutmeg, salt and white pepper. Continue cooking for 3–4 minutes until the liquid is absorbed. Remove from the heat and stir in the Parmesan and remaining butter.

6 Spoon into serving dishes and shave equal amounts of truffle over each portion. Drizzle over a little truffle oil, if using.

Beetroot, Dried Cherry & Red Wine Risotto

Serves 4–6

INGREDIENTS

175 g/6 oz dried sour cherries or
    dried cranberries

225 ml/8 fl oz fruity red wine,
    such as Valpolicella

3 tbsp olive oil

1 large red onion, finely chopped

2 sticks celery, finely chopped

½ tsp dried thyme

1 garlic clove, finely chopped

350 g/12 oz arborio or
    carnaroli rice

1.2 litres/2 pints chicken or
    vegetable stock, simmering

4 cooked beetroot (not in
    vinegar), diced

2 tbsp chopped fresh dill

2 tbsp fresh snipped chives

salt and pepper

60 g/2¼ oz freshly grated
    Parmesan cheese, to serve
    (optional)

1 Put the sour cherries in a saucepan with the wine and bring to the boil, then simmer for 2–3 minutes until slightly reduced. Remove from the heat and set aside.

2 Heat the olive oil in a large heavy-based saucepan over a medium heat. Add the onion, celery and thyme and cook for about 2 minutes until just beginning to soften. Add the garlic and rice and cook, stirring, until the rice is well coated.

3 Add a ladleful (about 225 ml/8 fl oz) of the simmering stock; it will bubble and steam rapidly. Cook, stirring constantly, until the stock is absorbed.

4 Continue adding the stock, about half a ladleful at a time, letting each addition be absorbed before adding the next – never let the rice cook 'dry'. This should take 20–25 minutes. The risotto should have a creamy consistency and the rice

should be tender, but firm to the bite.

5 Half way through the cooking time, remove the cherries from the wine with a slotted spoon and add to the risotto with the beetroot and half the wine. Continue adding the stock or remaining wine.

6 Stir in the dill and chives and season, if necessary. Serve with the Parmesan, if wished.

Courgette & Basil Risotto

Serves 4–6

INGREDIENTS

4 tbsp basil-flavoured extra-
    virgin olive oil, plus extra for
    drizzling
4 courgettes, diced
1 yellow pepper, cored, deseeded
    and diced
2 garlic cloves, finely chopped

1 large onion, finely chopped
400 g/14 oz arborio or
    carnaroli rice
80 ml/3 fl oz dry white vermouth
1.5 litres/2¾ pints chicken or
    vegetable stock, simmering

2 tbsp unsalted butter, at room
    temperature
large handful of fresh basil
    leaves, torn, plus a few leaves
    to garnish
85 g/3 oz freshly grated
    Parmesan cheese

1 Heat half the oil in a large frying pan over high heat. When very hot, but not smoking, add the courgettes and yellow pepper and stir-fry for 3 minutes until lightly golden. Stir in the garlic and cook for about 30 seconds longer. Transfer to a plate and set aside.

2 Heat the remaining oil in a large heavy-based saucepan over a medium heat. Add the chopped onion and cook for about 2 minutes until softened. Add the rice and cook, stirring frequently, for about 2 minutes until the rice is translucent and well coated with the oil.

3 Pour in the vermouth; it will bubble and steam rapidly and evaporate almost immediately. Add a ladleful (about 225 ml/8 fl oz) of the simmering stock and cook, stirring constantly until the stock is absorbed.

4 Continue adding the stock, about half a ladleful at a time, letting each addition be absorbed before adding the next. This should take 20–25 minutes. The risotto should have a creamy consistency and the rice should be tender, but still firm to the bite.

5 Stir in the courgette mixture with any juices, the butter, basil and Parmesan. Drizzle with a little oil and garnish with basil. Serve hot.

Wild Rocket & Tomato Risotto with Mozzarella

Serves 4–6

INGREDIENTS

2 tbsp olive oil
25 g/1 oz unsalted butter
1 large onion, finely chopped
2 garlic cloves, finely chopped
350 g/12 oz arborio rice
120 ml/4 fl oz dry white
  vermouth (optional)

1.5 litres/2¾ pints chicken or
  vegetable stock, simmering
6 vine-ripened or Italian plum
  tomatoes, deseeded and
  chopped
125 g/4½ oz wild rocket
handful of fresh basil leaves

115 g/4 oz/ freshly grated
  Parmesan cheese
225 g/8 oz fresh Italian buffalo
  mozzarella, coarsely grated
  or diced
salt and pepper

1 Heat the oil and half the butter in a large frying pan. Add the onion and cook for about 2 minutes until just beginning to soften. Stir in the garlic and rice and cook, stirring frequently, until the rice is translucent and well coated.

2 Pour in the white vermouth, if using; it will bubble and steam rapidly and evaporate almost immediately. Add a ladleful (about 225 ml/8 fl oz) of the simmering stock and cook, stirring constantly, until it is absorbed.

3 Continue adding the stock, about half a ladleful at a time, letting each addition be absorbed before adding the next – never let the rice cook 'dry'.

4 Just before the rice is tender, stir in the chopped tomatoes and rocket. Shred the basil leaves and immediately stir into the risotto. Continue to cook, adding more stock, until the risotto is creamy and the rice is tender, but firm to the bite.

5 Remove from the heat and stir in the remaining butter, the Parmesan and mozzarella. Season to taste with salt and pepper. Cover and stand for about 1 minute. Serve immediately, before the mozzarella melts completely.

Risotto with Sun-dried Tomatoes & Pecorino

Serves 6

INGREDIENTS

about 12 sun-dried tomatoes, not in oil
2 tbsp olive oil
1 large onion, finely chopped
4–6 garlic cloves, finely chopped

400 g/14 oz arborio or carnaroli rice
1.5 litres/2¾ pints chicken or vegetable stock, simmering

2 tbsp chopped fresh flat-leaved parsley
115 g/4 oz grated aged pecorino cheese
extra-virgin olive oil, for drizzling

1 Place the sun-dried tomatoes in a bowl and pour over enough boiling water to cover. Stand for about 30 minutes until soft and supple. Drain and pat dry, then shred thinly and set aside.

2 Heat the oil in a heavy-based saucepan over a medium heat. Add the onion and cook for about 2 minutes until beginning to soften. Add the garlic and cook for 15 seconds. Add the rice and cook, stirring frequently, for

2 minutes until the rice is translucent and well coated with oil.

3 Add a ladleful (about 225 ml/8 fl oz) of the hot stock; the stock will bubble and steam rapidly. Cook, stirring constantly, until the liquid is absorbed.

4 Continue adding the stock, about half a ladleful at a time, letting each addition be absorbed before adding the next – never let the rice cook 'dry'.

5 After about 15 minutes, stir in the sun-dried tomatoes. Continue to cook, adding the stock, until the rice is tender, but firm to the bite. The risotto should have a creamy consistency.

6 Remove from the heat and stir in the parsley and half the cheese. Cover, stand for about 1 minute, then spoon into serving dishes. Drizzle with extra-virgin olive oil and sprinkle the remaining cheese over the top. Serve immediately.

Orange-scented Risotto

Serves 4

INGREDIENTS

2 tbsp pine kernels
4 tbsp unsalted butter
2 shallots, finely chopped
1 leek, finely shredded
400 g/14 oz arborio or
   carnaroli rice

2 tbsp orange-flavoured liqueur
   or dry white vermouth
1.5 litres/2¾ pint chicken or
   vegetable stock, simmering
grated rind of 1 orange
juice of 2 oranges, strained

3 tbsp snipped fresh chives
salt and pepper

1 Toast the pine kernels in a frying pan over a medium heat for about 3 minutes, stirring and shaking frequently, until golden brown. Set aside.

2 Heat half the butter in a large heavy-based saucepan over a medium heat. Add the shallots and leek and cook for about 2 minutes until they begin to soften. Add the rice and cook, stirring frequently, for about 2 minutes until the rice is translucent and well coated with the butter.

3 Pour in the liqueur or vermouth; it will bubble and steam rapidly and evaporate almost immediately. Add a ladleful (about 225 ml/8 fl oz) of the hot stock and cook, stirring, until absorbed.

4 Continue adding the stock, about half a ladleful at a time, letting each addition be absorbed before adding the next – never let the rice cook 'dry'.

5 After about 15 minutes, add the orange rind and juice and continue to cook, adding more stock, until the rice is tender, but firm to the bite. The risotto should have a creamy consistency.

6 Remove from the heat and stir in the remaining butter and 2 tablespoons of the chives. Season with salt and pepper. Spoon into serving dishes and sprinkle with the toasted pine kernels and the remaining chives.

Black Cherry Risotto

Serves 6

INGREDIENTS

2 tbsp unblanched almonds

2 tbsp sunflower or vegetable oil

1 red onion, finely chopped

2 tbsp dried sour cherries
or raisins

450 g/1 lb black cherries or small
black plums, stoned

and halved

350 g/12 oz arborio or
arnaroli rice

225 ml/8 fl oz port or fruity
red wine

1.2 litres/2 pints chicken or
vegetable stock, simmering

50 ml/2 fl oz double cream
(optional)

2 tbsp chopped fresh chives, plus
whole chives for garnishing

salt and pepper

1 Lightly toast the almonds in a frying pan for about 2 minutes until golden. Cool, then chop roughly. Set aside.

2 Heat the oil in a large heavy-based saucepan over a medium heat. Add the onion and cook, stirring frequently, for about 2 minutes until beginning to soften. Add the dried cherries and the black cherries and stir for 2–3 minutes until the cherries begin to soften. Add the rice

to the pan and cook, stirring frequently, until the rice is translucent and well coated.

3 Pour in the port; it will bubble and steam rapidly. Cook, stirring, until it is absorbed. Add a ladleful (about 225 ml/8 fl oz) of the simmering stock and cook, stirring constantly until the stock is absorbed.

4 Continue adding the stock, about half a ladleful at a time, letting each addition be absorbed

before adding the next – never let the rice cook 'dry'. This should take 20–25 minutes. The risotto should have a creamy consistency and the rice should be tender, but still firm to the bite.

5 Stir in the cream, if using, and season with salt and pepper. Remove from the heat, stir in the chives and spoon into serving bowls. Sprinkle with the chopped almonds, garnish with the chives and serve immediately.

Crab Risotto with Roasted Peppers

Serves 4–6

INGREDIENTS

2–3 large red peppers
3 tbsp olive oil
1 onion, finely chopped
1 small fennel bulb, finely chopped
2 stalks celery, finely chopped
¼–½ tsp cayenne pepper, or to taste
350 g/12 oz arborio or carnaroli rice

800 g/1 lb 12 oz can Italian peeled
    plum tomatoes, drained and
    chopped
50 ml/2 fl oz dry white
    vermouth (optional)
1.5 litres/2¾ pints fish or light
    chicken stock, simmering

450 g/1 lb fresh cooked crab meat
    (white and dark meat)
50 ml/2 fl oz lemon juice
2–4 tbsp chopped fresh parsley
    or chervil
salt and pepper

1 Grill the peppers until the skins are charred. Transfer to a polythene bag and twist to seal. When cool enough to handle, peel off the charred skins, working over a bowl to catch the juices. Remove the cores and seeds; chop the flesh and set aside, reserving the juices.

2 Heat the olive oil in a large heavy-based saucepan. Add the onion, fennel and celery and cook for 2–3 minutes until the

vegetables are softened. Add the cayenne and rice and cook, stirring frequently, for about 2 minutes until the rice is translucent and well coated.

3 Stir in the tomatoes and vermouth, if using. The liquid will bubble and steam rapidly. When the liquid is almost absorbed, add a ladleful (about 225 ml/8 fl oz) of the simmering stock. Cook, stirring constantly, until the liquid is completely absorbed.

4 Continue adding the stock, about half a ladleful at a time, letting each addition be absorbed before adding the next. This should take 20–25 minutes. The risotto should have a creamy consistency and the rice should be tender, but firm to the bite.

5 Stir in the red peppers and juices, the crab meat, lemon juice and parsley or chervil and heat. Season with salt and pepper to taste. Serve immediately.

Risotto with Clams

Serves 6

INGREDIENTS

50 ml/2 fl oz olive oil
1 large onion, finely chopped
2 kg/4 lb 8 oz tiny clams, such as
    Venus, well scrubbed
125 ml/4 fl oz dry white wine
1 litre/1³/₄ pints fish stock

600 ml/1 pint water
3 garlic cloves, finely chopped
½ tsp crushed dried chilli
    (or to taste)
400 g/14 oz arborio or carnaroli
    rice

3 ripe plum tomatoes, skinned
    and coarsely chopped
3 tbsp lemon juice
2 tbsp chopped fresh chervil or
    parsley
salt and pepper

1 Heat 1–2 tablespoons of the oil in a large heavy-based saucepan over a medium-high heat. Add the onion and stir-fry for about 1 minute. Add the clams and wine and cover tightly. Cook for 2–3 minutes, shaking the pan frequently, until the clams begin to open. Remove from the heat and discard any clams that do not open.

2 When cool enough to handle, remove the clams from their shells. Rinse in the cooking liquid. Cover the clams and set aside. Strain the

cooking liquid through a paper coffee filter or a sieve lined with kitchen paper and reserve.

3 Bring the fish stock and water to the boil in a saucepan, then reduce the heat and keep at a gentle simmer.

4 Heat the remaining olive oil in a large, heavy-based saucepan over a medium heat. Add the garlic and chilli and cook gently for 1 minute. Add the rice and cook, stirring frequently, for about 2 minutes until translucent and well coated with oil.

5 Add a ladleful (about 225 ml /8 fl oz) of the simmering stock mixture; it will bubble and steam rapidly. Cook, stirring constantly, until the liquid is completely absorbed.

6 Continue adding the stock, about half a ladleful at a time, letting each addition be absorbed before adding the next – never let the rice cook 'dry'. This should take 20–25 minutes. The risotto should have a creamy consistency and the rice should be tender, but firm to the bite.

7 Stir in the tomatoes, reserved clams and their cooking liquid, the lemon juice and chervil. Heat through. Season to taste and serve immediately.

Black Risotto

Serves 6

INGREDIENTS

2–3 tbsp olive oil

450 g/1 lb cleaned squid or
    cuttlefish, cut crossways into
    thin strips, rinsed and
    patted dry

2 tbsp lemon juice

2 tbsp unsalted butter

3–4 garlic cloves, finely chopped

1 tsp crushed dried chilli, or
    to taste

350 g/12 oz arborio or
    carnaroli rice

125 ml/4 fl oz dry
    white wine

1 litre/1¾ pints fish stock,
    simmering

2 sachets squid or cuttlefish ink

2 tbsp chopped fresh flat-leaved
    parsley

salt and pepper

1 Heat half the olive oil in a large heavy-based frying pan over a medium-high heat. When the oil is very hot, add the squid strips and stir-fry for 2–3 minutes until just cooked. Transfer to a plate and sprinkle with the lemon juice.

2 Heat the remaining olive oil and butter in a large heavy-based pan over a medium heat. Add the garlic and chilli and cook gently for 1 minute. Add the rice and cook, stirring frequently, for about 2 minutes until translucent and well coated.

3 Pour in the white wine; it will bubble and steam rapidly. Cook, stirring frequently, until the wine is completely absorbed by the rice. Add a ladleful (about 225 ml/8 fl oz) of the simmering fish stock and cook, stirring constantly, until it is completely absorbed.

4 Continue adding the stock, about half a ladleful at a time, letting each addition be absorbed before adding the next – never let the rice cook 'dry'. This should take 20–25 minutes. The risotto should have a creamy consistency and the rice should be tender, but firm to the bite.

5 Just before adding the last ladleful of stock, add the squid ink to the stock and stir to blend completely. Stir into the risotto with the reserved squid pieces and the parsley. Season with salt and pepper to taste. Serve immediately.

Rich Lobster Risotto

Serves 4

INGREDIENTS

1 tbsp vegetable oil
4 tbsp unsalted butter
2 shallots, finely chopped
300 g/10½ oz arborio or
    carnaroli rice
½ tsp cayenne pepper, or to taste
80 ml/3 fl oz dry white vermouth

1.5 litres/2¾ pints shellfish, fish
    or light chicken stock,
    simmering
225 g/8 oz cherry tomatoes,
    quartered and deseeded
2–3 tbsp double or
    whipping cream

450 g/1 lb cooked lobster meat,
    cut into rough chunks
2 tbsp chopped fresh chervil
    or dill
salt and white pepper

1 Heat the oil and half the butter in a large heavy-based saucepan over a medium heat. Add the shallots and cook for about 2 minutes until just beginning to soften. Add the rice and cayenne pepper and cook, stirring frequently, for about 2 minutes until the rice is translucent and well coated with the oil and butter.

2 Pour in the vermouth; it will bubble and steam rapidly and evaporate almost immediately. Add a ladleful (about 225 ml/8 fl oz) of the simmering stock and cook, stirring constantly, until the stock is absorbed.

3 Continue adding the stock, about half a ladleful at a time, letting each addition be absorbed before adding the next – never let the rice cook 'dry'. This should take 20–25 minutes. The risotto should have a creamy consistency and the rice should be tender, but firm to the bite.

4 Stir in the tomatoes and cream and cook for about 2 minutes.

5 Add the cooked lobster meat, with the remaining butter and chervil, and cook long enough to just heat the lobster meat gently. Serve immediately.

Radicchio Risotto with Pancetta & Cream

Serves 6–8

INGREDIENTS

1 large head radicchio, outer damaged leaves removed	1 large onion, finely chopped	60 g/2¼ oz freshly grated Parmesan cheese
2 tbsp sunflower or other vegetable oil	1 garlic clove, finely chopped	3–4 tbsp chopped fresh flat-leaved parsley
2 tbsp unsalted butter	400 g/14 oz arborio or carnaroli rice	salt and pepper
115 g/4 oz pancetta or thick-cut smoky bacon, diced	1.5 litres/2¾ pints chicken or vegetable stock, simmering	fresh flat-leaved parsley sprigs, to garnish
	50 ml/2 fl oz double cream	

1 Cut the radicchio head in half lengthways; remove the triangular core. Place the halves cut-side down and shred finely. Set aside.

2 Heat the oil and butter in a heavy-based pan over a medium-high heat. Add the diced pancetta and cook for 3–4 minutes, stirring occasionally, until it begins to colour. Add the onion and garlic and cook for 1 minute, or until just beginning to soften.

3 Add the rice and cook, stirring frequently, for 2 minutes until translucent and well coated with the oil and butter. Stir in the radicchio for 1 minute until just beginning to wilt. Reduce the heat to medium.

4 Add a ladleful (about 225 ml/8 fl oz) of the simmering stock; the stock will bubble and steam rapidly. Cook, stirring constantly, until the stock is completely absorbed.

5 Continue adding the stock, about half a ladleful at a time, letting each addition be absorbed before adding the next. This should take 20–25 minutes. The risotto should have a creamy consistency and the rice should be tender, but firm to the bite.

6 Stir in the cream, Parmesan and parsley. Season with salt and pepper. Remove from the heat. Cover and stand for 1 minute. Garnish with parsley and serve.

Italian Sausage & Rosemary Risotto

Serves 4–6

INGREDIENTS

2 long sprigs fresh rosemary, plus
    extra to garnish
2 tbsp olive oil
4 tbsp unsalted butter
1 large onion, finely chopped
1 stick celery, finely chopped
2 garlic cloves, finely chopped

½ tsp dried thyme leaves
450 g/1 lb pork sausage such as
    luganega or Cumberland, cut
    into 1 cm/½ inch pieces
350 g/12 oz arborio or
    carnaroli rice
125 ml/4 fl oz fruity red wine

1.3 litres/2¼ pints chicken
    stock, simmering
85 g/3 oz freshly grated
    Parmesan cheese
salt and pepper

1 Strip the long thin leaves from the rosemary sprigs and chop finely; set aside.

2 Heat the oil and half the butter in a large heavy-based saucepan over a medium heat. Add the onion and celery and cook for about 2 minutes. Stir in the garlic, thyme, sausage and rosemary. Cook for about 5 minutes, stirring frequently, until the sausage begins to brown. Transfer the sausage to a plate.

3 Stir the rice into the pan and cook for about 2 minutes until the grains are translucent and coated with the butter and oil.

4 Pour in the red wine; it will bubble and steam rapidly and evaporate almost immediately. Add a ladleful (about 225 ml/8 fl oz) of the simmering stock and cook, stirring, until it is absorbed.

5 Continue adding the stock, about half a ladleful at a time, letting each addition be absorbed before adding the next. This should take 20–25 minutes. The risotto should have a creamy consistency and the rice should be tender, but firm to the bite.

6 Return the sausage pieces to the risotto and heat through. Remove from the heat; stir in the remaining butter and Parmesan. Season with salt and pepper. Cover, stand for about 1 minute, then garnish with rosemary. Serve.

Arrancini

Serves 6–8

INGREDIENTS

1 quantity Easy Cheesy Risotto
  with Parmesan (see page
  100), completely cooled
3 eggs
3 tbsp chopped fresh flat-leaved
  parsley

115 g/4 oz mozzarella, diced
vegetable oil, for frying
about 80 g/3 oz plain flour

about 100 g/3½ oz dried
  breadcrumbs, preferably
  homemade
salt and pepper

1 Put the risotto in a large mixing bowl and stir to break up. Beat 2 of the eggs lightly, then gradually beat enough into the risotto until the risotto begins to stick together. Beat in the parsley.

2 Using wet hands, form the mixture into balls about the size of a large egg.

3 Poke a hole in the centre of each ball and fill with a few cubes of the mozzarella. Carefully seal the hole over with the risotto mixture. Place on a large baking sheet.

4 In a deep-fat fryer or large heavy-based saucepan, heat about 7.5 cm/3 inches of oil to 180–190°C/350–375°F or until a cube of bread browns.

5 Spread the flour on a large plate and season with salt and pepper. In a bowl, beat the remaining egg and add any unused egg from Step 1. Spread the breadcrumbs on another large plate and season with salt and pepper.

6 Roll each risotto ball in a little seasoned flour,

shaking off the excess. Carefully coat in the egg, then roll in the breadcrumbs to coat completely.

7 Deep fry 3–4 balls for about 2 minutes until crisp and golden, then transfer to kitchen paper to drain. Keep hot in a warm oven while frying the remaining balls. Serve immediately while the cheese is still soft and melted.

Frittata Risotto

Serves 4–6

INGREDIENTS

about 80 ml/3 fl oz olive oil
1 large red onion, finely chopped
1 red pepper, cored, deseeded and chopped
1 garlic clove, finely chopped

3–4 sun-dried tomatoes, finely shredded
2 tbsp chopped fresh flat-leaved parsley or basil
1 quantity Easy Cheesy Risotto

with Parmesan (see page 100) or Risotto alla Milanese (see page 156), cooled
about 60 g/2¼ oz freshly grated Parmesan cheese

1 Heat 2 tablespoons of the oil in a large heavy-based frying pan over a medium-high heat. Add the onion and red pepper and cook for 3–4 minutes until the vegetables are soft.

2 Add the garlic and sun-dried tomatoes and cook for 2 minutes. Remove from the heat. Stir in the parsley; cool slightly.

3 Put the risotto in a bowl and break up with a fork. Stir in the vegetable mixture with half the Parmesan. Stir to mix well.

4 Reserve 1 tablespoon of the remaining oil and heat the rest in the cleaned frying pan over a medium heat. Remove from the heat and spoon in the risotto mixture, pressing it into an even cake-like layer, about 2–2.5 cm/¾–1 inch thick. Return to the heat and cook for about 4 minutes until crisp and brown on the bottom.

5 With a palette knife, loosen the edges and give the pan a shake. Slide the frittata on to a large plate. Protecting your hands, invert the frying pan over the frittata and, holding both firmly together, flip them over. Return to the heat and drizzle the remaining oil around the edge of the frittata, gently pulling the edges towards the centre with the palette knife. Cook for 1–2 minutes to seal the bottom, then slide on to a serving plate.

6 Sprinkle the top with some of the remaining Parmesan. Cut into wedges and serve with the rest of the Parmesan.

Cheese-topped Risotto Tart with Spinach

Serves 6–8

INGREDIENTS

190 g/6½ oz plain flour
½ tsp salt
1 tsp caster sugar
115 g/4 oz unsalted
 butter, diced
1 egg yolk, beaten with 2 tbsp
 iced water

FILLING
1 quantity Easy Cheesy Risotto
 with Parmesan (see
 page 100), still warm
250 g/9 oz spinach, cooked,
 drained very well and
 chopped

2 tbsp double cream
225 g/8 oz mozzarella, preferably
 buffalo
85 g/3 oz freshly grated
 Parmesan cheese

1 To make the shortcrust pastry sift the flour, salt and sugar into a large bowl and sprinkle over the butter. Rub the butter into the flour until the mixture forms coarse crumbs. Sprinkle in the egg mixture and stir to make a dough.

2 Gather the dough into a ball, wrap in cling film and chill for at least 1 hour.

3 Gently roll out the pastry to a thickness of about 3 mm/⅛ inch, then use to line a lightly greased tart tin (23–25 cm/ 9–10 inch) with a removable base. Prick the bottom with a fork and chill for 1 hour.

4 Cover the tart case with baking parchment and fill with baking beans. Bake blind in a preheated oven at 200°C/400°F/Gas Mark 6 for about 20 minutes until the pastry is set and the edge is golden. Remove the beans and parchment and set aside. Reduce the oven temperature to 180°C/350°F/Gas Mark 4.

5 Put the risotto in a bowl and stir in the spinach, cream, half the mozzarella and half the Parmesan. Spoon into the tart case and smooth the top. Sprinkle evenly with the remaining cheeses.

6 Bake for 12–15 minutes or until cooked through and golden. Remove the tart from the oven, cool slightly on a wire rack, then serve warm.

Oven-baked Risotto with Mushrooms

Serves 4–6

INGREDIENTS

4 tbsp olive oil

400 g/14 oz portobello or large field mushrooms, thickly sliced

115 g/4 oz pancetta or thick-cut smoky bacon, diced

1 large onion, finely chopped

2 garlic cloves, finely chopped

350 g/12 oz arborio or carnaroli rice

1.2 litres/2 pints chicken stock, simmering

2 tbsp chopped fresh tarragon or flat-leaved parsley

85 g/3 oz freshly grated Parmesan cheese, plus extra for sprinkling

salt and pepper

1 Heat 2 tablespoons of the oil in a large heavy-based frying pan over a high heat. Add the mushrooms and stir-fry for 2–3 minutes until golden and tender-crisp. Transfer to a plate.

2 Add the pancetta to the pan and cook for about 2 minutes, stirring frequently, until crisp and golden. Add to the mushrooms on the plate.

3 Heat the remaining oil in a heavy-based saucepan over a medium heat. Add the onion and cook for about 2 minutes until beginning to soften. Add the garlic and rice and cook, stirring, for about 2 minutes until the rice is well coated with the oil.

4 Gradually stir the stock into the rice, then add the mushroom and pancetta mixture and the tarragon. Season with salt and pepper. Bring to the boil.

5 Remove from the heat and transfer to a casserole.

6 Cover and bake in a preheated oven at 180°C/350°F/Gas Mark 4 for about 20 minutes until the rice is almost tender and most of the liquid is absorbed. Uncover and stir in the Parmesan. Continue to bake for about 15 minutes longer until the rice is tender, but still firm to the bite. Serve at once with extra Parmesan for sprinkling.

Famous Rice Dishes

In this chapter, you can travel the world and sample some of the traditional and delectable rice dishes that have evolved in the various rice-producing countries over hundreds of years, using a blend of exotic flavours and ingredients.

For a flavour of Europe, try your hand at making a Spanish Paella, a wonderful mix of chicken, shellfish and rice, or serve the delicately flavoured Greek Egg & Lemon Soup as a light lunch. Travelling to the Middle East, savour an unusual, spicy lamb and rice sausage, Mumbar, or learn how to make delicious Mujadarah, a marvellous combination of rice, lentils and caramelized onions.

Capture the exotic flavours of India with Murgh Pullau, a fragrant chicken and almond pilaf, or discover the delights of Thai cooking with spicy red pork curry with jasmine-scented rice. Popular Chinese Fried Rice is a must to try at home and the classic fried rice dish of Indonesia, Nasi Goreng, a medley of Far-Eastern flavours, is ideal for any occasion. Vietnamese Spring Rolls are a culinary treat and fun to eat, while for entertaining, Japanese Sushi make stunning fare.

Risotto alla Milanese

Serves 4–6

INGREDIENTS

½–1 tsp saffron threads
1.3 litres/2¼ pints chicken
    stock, simmering
6 tbsp unsalted butter

2–3 shallots, finely chopped
400 g/14 oz arborio or
    carnaroli rice

175 g/6 oz freshly grated
    Parmesan cheese
salt and pepper

1 Put the saffron threads in a small bowl. Pour over enough of the stock to cover the threads, then set aside to infuse.

2 Melt 2 tablespoons of the butter in a large heavy-based pan over a medium heat. Add the shallots and cook for about 2 minutes until beginning to soften. Add the rice and cook, stirring frequently, for about 2 minutes until the rice is beginning to turn translucent and is well coated.

3 Add a ladleful (about 225 ml/8 fl oz) of the simmering stock; it will steam and bubble rapidly. Cook, stirring constantly, until the liquid is absorbed.

4 Continue adding the stock, about half a ladleful at a time, letting each addition be absorbed before adding the next – never let the rice cook 'dry'.

5 After about 15 minutes, stir in the saffron-infused stock; the rice will turn a vibrant yellow and the colour will become deeper as it cooks. Continue cooking, adding the stock in the same way until the rice is tender, but still firm to the bite. The risotto should have a creamy porridge-like consistency.

6 Stir in the remaining butter and half the Parmesan, then remove from the heat. Cover and stand for about 1 minute.

7 Spoon the risotto into serving bowls and serve immediately with the remaining Parmesan.

Dolmades

Serves 10–12

INGREDIENTS

115 g/4 oz/about 24 large vine leaves, packed in brine, drained	¾ tsp dried oregano	2 tbsp chopped fresh mint
olive oil	½ tsp ground cinnamon	1 tbsp chopped fresh flat-leaved parsley
1 onion, finely chopped	200 g/7 oz long-grain white rice	4 tbsp lemon juice
2 garlic cloves, finely chopped	350 ml/12 fl oz water	350 ml/12 fl oz chicken stock
¾ tsp dried thyme	2 tsp raisins	salt and pepper
	2 tbsp pine kernels, lightly toasted	

1 Cover the vine leaves with boiling water and leave for 2 minutes. Drain, rinse and pat dry. Cut off any thick stems. Place shiny-side down on kitchen paper.

2 Heat 2 tablespoons of the olive oil in a heavy-based pan. Add the onion and cook for about 3 minutes until soft. Stir in the garlic, dried herbs and cinnamon, then add the rice and cook for about 2 minutes, stirring, until translucent and coated with the oil.

3 Stir in the water and raisins and bring to the boil, stirring twice. Simmer, covered tightly, for 15 minutes until the liquid is absorbed and the rice just tender.

4 Fork the rice into a bowl and add the pine kernels, mint, parsley and half the lemon juice. Stir and season with salt and pepper and 1 tablespoon olive oil.

5 Place about 1 tablespoon of the rice mixture on a vine leaf near the stem end and roll the leaf once over the filling. Fold in each side of the leaf, then finish rolling. Repeat with the remaining leaves.

6 Brush a large deep flameproof dish or casserole with about 2 tablespoons of olive oil. Arrange the dolmades tightly in 2 rows, making a second layer if necessary. Sprinkle with another tablespoon of the oil and the remaining lemon juice. Add the stock to cover the rolls; add extra water if necessary to make enough liquid.

7 Weight down the rolls with a heatproof plate, cover tightly with a lid or kitchen foil and cook over a very low heat for about 1 hour. Remove from the heat and let cool to room temperature. Drain and serve with a little of the cooking juices, if wished.

Mujadarah

Serves 4

INGREDIENTS

225 g/8 oz green or brown
   lentils, rinsed
125 g/4 fl oz olive oil
3 large onions, thinly sliced
200 g/7 oz basmati or
   long-grain white rice

700 ml/1¼ pints light chicken
   or vegetable stock
1 tsp ground allspice or ground
   cinnamon
salt and pepper

TO SERVE
lemon wedges
spring onions, thinly sliced
   on the diagonal
natural yogurt

1 Bring a large saucepan of water to the boil. Gradually pour in the lentils (so the water remains boiling). Reduce the heat to medium-low and simmer for about 25 minutes, skimming off any foam that rises to the surface, until just tender. Drain the lentils and set aside (see Cook's Tip).

2 Meanwhile, heat the oil in a large, deep frying pan over a medium heat until very hot. Add the onions and cook for 4–5 minutes until soft. Using a slotted spoon, transfer about two-thirds of the onions to a bowl; set aside. Continue cooking the remaining onions until brown and crisp, then drain on kitchen paper.

3 Add the rice to the pan and cook, stirring frequently, for about 2 minutes until translucent and well coated with the oil. Add the less-cooked onions, with the lentils and stock and stir gently, scraping the base of the pan to release any crispy bits. Add the ground allspice and season with salt and pepper.

4 Tightly cover the pan and cook over a very low heat for about 20 minutes until the rice is tender and all the stock is absorbed. Fork the rice mixture into a serving bowl; top with the crispy onions. Serve with lemon wedges, spring onions and yogurt.

COOK'S TIP

If preferred, reserve the lentil cooking liquid and use instead of the chicken or vegetable stock.

Greek Egg & Lemon Soup

Serves 6–8

INGREDIENTS

1.5 litres/2¾ pints chicken or
lamb stock
75–100 g/2¾–3½ oz long-grain
white rice

3 eggs, separated
3–4 tbsp lemon juice
1 tbsp water
salt and white pepper

1 tbsp chopped fresh flat-leaved
parsley, to garnish (optional)

1 Bring the stock to the boil in a large saucepan. Add the rice in a very slow stream so the stock does not stop boiling; stir once or twice. Reduce the heat and simmer gently, partially covered, until the rice is tender; skim off any foam which rises to the surface.

2 Whisk the egg whites in a large bowl until almost stiff.

3 Add the egg yolks and continue whisking until the mixture is light and creamy. Gradually beat in the lemon juice and water.

4 Gradually whisk in half of the hot stock and rice, about 2 tablespoons at a time. Be careful to add the hot stock very slowly to the egg and lemon mixture, and whisk constantly, otherwise the eggs may curdle.

5 Remove the remaining stock and rice from the heat, transfer to a bowl and gradually whisk in the egg and stock mixture. Continue to whisk for 1 minute to let the stock cool slightly. Season with salt and pepper and serve immediately. Garnish with a little chopped parsley, if wished.

COOK'S TIP

Using a food processor can help prevent the egg and lemon mixture from curdling. Add the egg whites to a food processor fitted with the metal blade and process for about 1 minute until very thick and foamy. Add the egg yolks and continue to process for 1 minute. With the machine running, gradually pour the lemon and water through the feed tube until combined. Continue from Step 4.

Kedgeree

Serves 4–6

INGREDIENTS

700 g/1 lb 9 oz thick, undyed
smoked haddock or cod fillets
milk, for poaching
2 bay leaves
1 tbsp vegetable oil
4 tbsp butter
1 onion, finely chopped

1 tsp hot curry powder, or to taste
1 tsp dry mustard powder
300 g/10½ oz basmati rice
750 ml/1½ pints water
2 small leeks, trimmed and cut
into 5 mm/¼ inch slices

2 tbsp chopped fresh flat-leaved
parsley or coriander
a squeeze of lemon juice
3–4 hard-boiled eggs, peeled
and quartered
salt and pepper
lemon quarters, to serve

1 Put the fish in a frying pan and pour in enough milk to just cover; add the bay leaves. Bring to the boil, then simmer gently, covered, for about 4 minutes. Remove from the heat and stand, covered, for about 10 minutes.

2 Using a slotted spoon, transfer the fish to a plate and cover loosely; set aside. Reserve the cooking milk, discarding the bay leaves.

3 Heat the oil and half the butter in a large pan over a medium heat. Add the onion and cook for about 2 minutes until soft. Stir in the curry powder and the mustard powder and cook for 1 minute.

4 Add the rice and stir for about 2 minutes until well coated. Add the water and bring to the boil; stir and reduce the heat to very low. Cook, covered, for 20–25 minutes until the rice is tender and the water absorbed.

5 Melt the remaining butter in a flameproof casserole, add the leeks and cook for about 4 minutes until soft. Fork the leeks into the hot rice. Add 2–3 tablespoons of the reserved milk to moisten.

6 Flake the fish off the skin into large pieces and fold into the rice. Stir in the parsley and lemon juice, then season with salt and pepper. Add a little more milk, if wished, then add the egg quarters. Serve, with lemon quarters.

Spanish Paella

Serves 4

INGREDIENTS

125 ml/4 fl oz olive oil
1.5 kg/3 lb 5 oz chicken, cut into 8 pieces
350 g/12 oz chorizo sausage, cut into 1 cm/½ inch pieces
115 g/4 oz cured ham, chopped
2 onions, finely chopped
2 red peppers, cored, deseeded and cut into 2.5 cm/1 inch pieces

4–6 garlic cloves
750 g/1lb 10 oz short-grain Spanish rice or Italian arborio rice
2 bay leaves
1 tsp dried thyme
1 tsp saffron threads
225 ml/8 fl oz dry white wine
1.5 litres/2¾ pints chicken stock
115 g/4 oz fresh or frozen peas

450 g/1 lb medium uncooked prawns
8 raw King prawns, in shells
16 clams, very well scrubbed
16 mussels, very well scrubbed
salt and pepper
4 tbsp chopped fresh flat-leaved parsley

1 Heat half the oil in a 46 cm/18 inch paella pan or deep, wide frying pan over a medium-high heat. Add the chicken and fry gently, turning, until golden brown. Remove from the pan and set aside.

2 Add the chorizo and ham to the pan and cook for about 7 minutes, stirring occasionally, until crisp. Remove and set aside.

3 Stir the onions into the pan and cook for about 3 minutes until soft. Add the peppers and garlic and cook until beginning to soften; remove and set aside.

4 Add the remaining oil to the pan and stir in the rice until well coated. Add the bay leaves, thyme and saffron and stir well. Pour in the wine, bubble, then pour in the stock, stirring well and scraping the bottom of the pan. Bring to the boil, stirring often.

5 Stir in the cooked vegetables. Add the chorizo, ham and chicken and gently bury in the rice. Reduce the heat and cook for 10 minutes, stirring occasionally.

6 Add the peas and prawns and cook for a further 5 minutes. Push the clams and mussels into the rice. Cover and cook over a very low heat for about 5 minutes until the rice is tender and the shellfish open. Discard any unopened clams or mussels. Season to taste.

7 Remove from the heat, and stand, covered, for about 5 minutes. Sprinkle with parsley and serve.

Salmon Coulibiac

Serves 4

INGREDIENTS

115 g/4 oz butter, plus extra
2 tbsp butter (melted)
2 onions, finely chopped
115 g/4 oz long-grain white rice
750 g/1 lb 10 oz skinned salmon
fillet, poached in water,
cooking liquid reserved

150 g/5½ oz mushrooms, thinly
sliced
85 g/3 oz cooked spinach,
chopped
2 tbsp chopped fresh dill
6 canned anchovy fillets in oil,
drained and chopped
5 hard-boiled eggs, chopped

grated rind and juice of 1 large
lemon
375 g/13 oz packet puff pastry
1 egg, beaten, for glaze
salt and pepper
lemon wedges and dill sprigs, to
garnish

1 Melt half of the butter in a large saucepan, add half the onion and cook for about 2 minutes until soft. Stir in the rice for 2 minutes until well coated.

2 If necessary, add water to the reserved fish cooking liquid to make up to 225 ml/ 8 fl oz. Add to the rice, bring to the boil, then cover and cook very gently for about 18 minutes. Allow to cool.

3 Melt the remaining butter in a frying pan,

add the remaining onions and mushrooms and cook for about 8 minutes until there is no liquid. Add the spinach and dill. Season well, then let cool.

4 Add the anchovies, eggs and lemon rind and juice to the mushroom mixture and toss well.

5 Roll out the puff pastry and cut into two squares, one 28 cm/11 inches square and the other 30 cm/ 12 inches square. Place the

smaller piece on a lightly greased baking sheet and spread half the mushroom mixture over, leaving a 2.5 cm/1 inch border; spoon over half the rice.

6 Centre the salmon on top of the rice layer and cover with the remaining rice. Spoon the remaining mushrooms over. Drizzle the melted butter over the top. Brush the pastry edges with egg, cover with the second square and seal the edges.

7 Brush with egg and mark a lattice pattern on top. Bake in a preheated oven 220°C/425°F/Gas Mark 7 for about 35 minutes until golden. Rest on a wire rack, then serve garnished.

Stuffed Cabbage

Serves 6–8

INGREDIENTS

60 g/2¼ oz fresh white
breadcrumbs
125 ml/4 fl oz milk
1 tbsp vegetable oil
1 onion, finely chopped
2 garlic cloves, finely chopped
450 g/1 lb minced beef steak
450 g/1 lb minced pork or veal
2 tbsp tomato ketchup
3 tbsp chopped fresh dill

1 tsp chopped fresh thyme leaves
100 g/3½ oz long-grain white
rice
salt and pepper
1 large cabbage, such as Savoy,
leaves separated and
blanched

TOMATO SAUCE
2 tbsp olive oil

2 large onions, thinly sliced
800g/1lb 12oz canned chopped
tomatoes
450 ml/16 fl oz sieved tomatoes
or passata
50 ml/2 fl oz tomato ketchup
grated rind and juice of 1 large
lemon
2 tbsp light brown sugar
75 g/2¾ oz raisins

1 Combine the breadcrumbs and the milk; leave to soak. Heat the oil and cook the onion and garlic in the oil for about 2 minutes until soft, then set aside.

2 Place the beef and pork in a bowl. Mix in the ketchup, herbs, rice and seasoning. Add the breadcrumbs, cooked onion and garlic.

3 To make the tomato sauce, heat the oil and cook the onions for 3 minutes until soft. Stir in the tomatoes and the remaining ingredients and bring to the boil, then simmer for about 15 minutes, stirring occasionally. Set aside.

4 To fill the leaves, spoon 1–2 tablespoons of the meat mixture on to a cabbage leaf above the stem end. Fold the stem end over the filling,

then fold over the sides. Roll up to enclose. Repeat with the remaining leaves.

5 Spoon enough tomato sauce to cover the base of a large baking dish. Arrange the filled cabbage rolls, seam-side down, in the dish. Spoon the remaining sauce over the rolls to just cover – add a little water if necessary. Cover tightly and bake in a preheated oven at 160°C/325°F/Gas Mark 3 for about 1½ hours, basting once or twice.

6 Transfer the cabbage rolls to a serving plate and keep warm. Bubble the sauce to thicken, if necessary. Serve at once.

Mediterranean Stuffed Peppers

Serves 6

INGREDIENTS

6 large peppers, red, yellow and orange	2 garlic cloves, finely chopped	50 ml/2 fl oz white wine
200 g/7 oz long-grain white rice	1/2 tsp ground cinnamon or allspice	4 anchovy fillets, chopped
2-3 tbsp olive oil, plus extra for greasing and drizzling	75 g/2¾ oz raisins	1/2 bunch chopped fresh parsley
1 large onion	4 tbsp pine kernels, lightly toasted	1/2 bunch chopped fresh mint
2 sticks celery, chopped	4 ripe plum tomatoes, deseeded and chopped	6 tbsp freshly grated Parmesan cheese
		salt and pepper
		fresh tomato sauce– see page 170

1 Using a sharp knife, slice off the tops of the peppers, then remove the cores and seeds. Blanch the peppers in boiling water for 2–3 minutes. Carefully remove and drain upside-down on a wire rack.

2 Bring a saucepan of salted water to the boil. Gradually pour in the rice and return to the boil; simmer until tender, but firm to the bite. Drain and rinse under cold running water. Set aside.

3 Heat the oil in a large frying pan. Add the onion and celery and cook for 2 minutes. Stir in the garlic, cinnamon and raisins and cook for 1 minute. Fork in the rice, then stir in the pine kernels, tomatoes, wine, anchovies, parsley and mint and cook for 4 minutes. Remove from the heat, add salt and pepper and stir in half the Parmesan.

4 Brush the bottom of a baking dish with a little oil. Divide the rice mixture equally among the peppers. Arrange in the dish and sprinkle with the remaining Parmesan. Drizzle with a little more oil and pour in enough water to come 1 cm/ ½ inch up the sides of the peppers. Loosely cover the dish with kitchen foil.

5 Bake in a preheated oven at 180°C/350°F/ Gas Mark 4 for about 40 minutes. Uncover and cook for a further 10 minutes. Serve hot with tomato sauce.

Jamaican Rice and Peas

Serves 6–8

INGREDIENTS

450 g/1 lb dried beans, such as
black-eyed beans, black beans
or small red kidney beans,
soaked in cold water overnight
2 tbsp vegetable oil
1 large onion, chopped
2–3 garlic cloves, finely chopped
2 red chillies, deseeded and
chopped

450 g/1 lb long-grain white rice
400 ml/14 fl oz canned coconut
milk
³/₄ tsp dried thyme
about 1 teaspoon salt

TOMATO SALSA
4 ripe tomatoes, deseeded and
cut into 5 mm/¹/₄ inch dice

1 red onion, finely chopped
4 tbsp chopped fresh coriander
2 garlic cloves, finely chopped
1–2 jalapeño chillies, or to taste,
deseeded and thinly sliced
1–2 tbsp extra-virgin olive oil
1 tbsp fresh lime juice
1 tsp light brown sugar
salt and pepper

1 Drain the soaked beans, rinse and put in a large pan. Cover with cold water by about 5 cm/2 inches and bring to the boil, over a high heat, skimming off any foam.

2 Boil the beans for about 10 minutes (to remove any toxins), drain and rinse again. Return to the pan, cover with cold water again and bring to the boil over a high heat.

3 Reduce the heat and keep at a moderate simmer,

partially covered, for about 1¼–1½ hours for black-eyed beans, 1½–2 hours for black beans or 50–60 minutes for kidney beans, until tender. Drain, reserving the cooking liquid.

4 Heat the oil in another pan. Add the onion and cook for about 2 minutes until soft. Stir in the garlic and chillies and cook for a further minute. Add the rice and stir until well coated.

5 Stir in the coconut milk, thyme and salt. Add the cooked beans and 450 ml/ 16 fl oz of the reserved bean cooking liquid to cover; add more bean liquid if necessary. Bring the mixture to the boil, then reduce the heat to low, cover tightly and cook for 20–25 minutes.

6 Meanwhile, make the tomato salsa: combine all the ingredients in a bowl and stand, loosely covered, at room temperature.

7 Remove the rice from the heat and stand, covered, for 5 minutes, then fork into a serving bowl. Serve hot with the salsa.

Creole Jambalaya

Serves 6–8

INGREDIENTS

2 tbsp vegetable oil

85 g/3 oz piece good-quality smoked ham, cut into bite-sized pieces

85 g/3 oz andouille or pure smoked pork sausage, such as Polish kielbasa, cut into chunks

2 large onions, finely chopped

3–4 sticks celery, finely chopped

2 green peppers, cored, deseeded and finely chopped

2 garlic cloves, finely chopped

225 g/8 oz boned chicken breast or thighs, skinned and cut into pieces

4 ripe tomatoes, skinned and chopped

175 ml/6 fl oz cup passata or sieved strained tomatoes

450 ml/16 fl oz fish stock

400 g/14 oz long-grain white rice

4 spring onions, cut into 2.5 cm/ 1 inch pieces

250 g/9 oz peeled raw prawns, tails on, if wished

250 g/9 oz cooked white crab meat

12 oysters, shelled, with their liquor

SEASONING MIX

2 dried bay leaves

1 tsp salt

1½–2 tsp cayenne pepper, or to taste

1½ tsp dried oregano

1 tsp ground white and black pepper, or to taste

1 To make the seasoning mix, mix the ingredients in a bowl.

2 Heat the oil in a flame-proof casserole over a medium heat. Add the smoked ham and the sausage and cook for about 8 minutes, stirring frequently, until golden. Using a slotted spoon, transfer to a large plate.

3 Add the onions, celery and peppers to the casserole and cook for about 4 minutes until just softened. Stir in the garlic, then remove and set aside.

4 Add the chicken pieces to the casserole and cook for 3–4 minutes until beginning to colour. Stir in the seasoning mix to coat.

5 Return the ham, sausage and vegetables to the casserole and stir to combine. Add the chopped tomatoes and passata, then pour in the stock. Bring to the boil.

6 Stir in the rice and simmer for about 12 minutes. Stir in the spring onions and prawns and cook, covered, for 4 minutes.

7 Add the crab meat and oysters with their liquor. Cook until the rice is just tender, and the oysters slightly firm. Remove from the heat. Stand, covered, for 3 minutes before serving.

Murgh Pullau

Serves 4–6

INGREDIENTS

350 g/12 oz basmati rice

4 tbsp ghee or butter

115 g/4 oz flaked almonds

85 g/3 oz unsalted, shelled
pistachio nuts

4–6 boned chicken breasts,
skinned and each cut into 4
pieces

2 onions, thinly sliced

2 garlic cloves, chopped finely

2.5 cm/1 inch piece fresh ginger
root, peeled and chopped

6 green cardamom pods, lightly
crushed

4–6 whole cloves

2 bay leaves

1 tsp ground coriander

½ tsp cayenne pepper

225 ml/8 fl oz natural yogurt

125 ml/4 fl oz boiling water

225 ml/8 fl oz double cream

2–4 tbsp chopped fresh coriander
or mint

225 g/8 oz seedless green grapes,
halved if large

1 Bring a saucepan of salted water to the boil. Gradually pour in the rice, return to the boil, then simmer until the rice is just tender. Drain and rinse under cold running water; set aside.

2 Heat the ghee in a deep frying pan over a medium-high heat. Add the almonds and pistachios and cook for 3 minutes, stirring, until light golden. Remove and reserve.

3 Add the chicken to the pan and cook for about 5 minutes, turning, until golden. Remove and reserve. Add the onions to the pan. Cook for about 10 minutes until golden. Stir in the garlic and spices and cook for 3 minutes.

4 Add 2–3 tablespoons of the yogurt and cook, stirring, until all the moisture evaporates. Continue adding the rest of the yogurt in the same way.

5 Return the chicken and nuts to the pan and stir to coat. Stir in the water. Season with salt and pepper and cook, covered, over a low heat for about 10 minutes until the chicken is cooked through. Stir in the cream, coriander and grapes and remove from the heat.

6 Fork the rice into a bowl, then gently fold in the chicken and sauce. Stand for 5 minutes. Serve.

Mumbar

Serves 6–8

INGREDIENTS

100 g/3½ oz basmati rice
900 g/2 lb finely minced lamb
1 small onion, finely chopped
3–4 garlic cloves, crushed
1 bunch each flat-leaved parsley
    and coriander finely chopped
2–3 tbsp tomato ketchup
1 tbsp vegetable oil

pared rind and juice of 1 lime
700 ml /1¼ pints hot lamb stock
salt and pepper

BAHARAT SEASONING MIX
2 tbsp black peppercorns
1 tbsp coriander seeds
2 tsp whole cloves

1½ tsp cumin seeds
1 tsp cardamom seeds
1 cinnamon stick, broken into
    small pieces
1 whole nutmeg
2 tbsp hot paprika

1 To make the baharat, grind the first 6 ingredients into a fine powder. Grate the whole nutmeg into the mix and stir in the paprika. Store in an airtight jar.

2 Bring a pan of salted water to the boil. Pour in the rice, return to the boil, then simmer until the rice is tender, but firm to the bite. Drain and rinse.

3 Place the lamb in a large bowl and break up with a fork. Add the onion, garlic, parsley, coriander, ketchup and 1 teaspoon of the baharat. Stir in the cooked rice and season. Squeeze the mixture to make it pastelike.

4 Divide into 4-6 pieces and roll each into a sausage of 2.5cm/1 inch thick. Brush a 23–25 cm/9–10 inch frying pan with the oil. Starting in the centre of the pan, coil the sausage pieces, joining each piece, to form one long coiled sausage.

5 Press lightly to make an even layer, then tuck the lime rind between the spaces of the sausage. Add the lime juice to the pan. Pour in the hot stock and cover with a plate to keep in place.

6 Bring to the boil, then simmer gently for about 10 minutes. Cover; continue to cook for 15 minutes. Remove from the heat, drain and slide the sausage on to a serving plate. Sprinkle with a little more of the baharat to serve.

Lamb Biriyani

Serves 4

INGREDIENTS

900 g/2 lb boned lean leg or
    shoulder of lamb, cut into
    2.5 cm/1 inch cubes
6 garlic cloves, finely chopped
4 cm/1½ inch piece fresh ginger
    root, peeled and finely chopped
1 tbsp ground cinnamon
1 tbsp green cardamom pods,
    crushed to expose the black
    seeds
1 tsp whole cloves
2 tsp coriander seeds, crushed

2 tsp cumin seeds, crushed
½ tsp ground turmeric (optional)
2 fresh green chillies, deseeded
    and chopped
grated rind and juice of 1 lime
1 bunch fresh coriander, chopped
    finely
1 bunch fresh mint, chopped
    finely
125 ml/4 fl oz natural yogurt
115 g/4 oz ghee, butter or
    vegetable oil

4 onions, 3 thinly sliced and
    1 finely chopped
about 225 ml/8 fl oz water
600 g/1 lb 5 oz basmati rice
2 cinnamon sticks, broken
½ tsp nutmeg, freshly grated
3–4 tbsp raisins
1.2 litres/2 pints chicken stock
    or water
225 ml/8 fl oz hot milk
1 tsp saffron threads
salt and pepper

1 Combine the lamb, garlic, ginger, cinnamon, cardamom, cloves, coriander and cumin seeds, turmeric, chillies, lime rind and juice, 2 tablespoons each of coriander and mint and yogurt. Marinate for 2–3 hours.

2 Heat about half the fat in a large frying pan, add the sliced onions and cook for about 8 minutes until lightly browned. Add the meat and any juices; season with salt and pepper. Stir in the water and simmer for 18–20 minutes until the lamb is just cooked.

3 Meanwhile, heat the fat left over in a flameproof casserole. Add the chopped onion and cook for 2 minutes until soft. Add the rice and cook, stirring, for 3–4 minutes until well coated. Add the cinnamon, nutmeg, raisins and stock. Bring to the boil, stirring once or twice, and season with salt and pepper. Simmer, covered, over a low heat for 12 minutes until the liquid is reduced but the rice is still a little firm.

4 Pour the hot milk over the saffron; stand for 10 minutes. Remove the rice from the heat and stir in the saffron-milk. Fold in the lamb mixture. Cover and bake in a preheated oven at 350°C/180°F/Gas Mark 4 until the rice is cooked and the liquid absorbed.

Red Pork Curry with Jasmine-scented Rice

Serves 4–6

INGREDIENTS

900 g/2 lb boned pork shoulder, cut into thin slices

700 ml/1¼ pints coconut milk

2 fresh red chillies, deseeded and thinly sliced

2 tbsp Thai fish sauce

2 tsp brown sugar

1 large red pepper, cored, deseeded and thinly sliced

6 kaffir lime leaves, shredded

½ bunch fresh mint leaves, shredded

½ bunch Thai basil leaves or Italian-style basil, shredded

jasmine-scented or Thai fragrant rice, cooked according to the packet instructions and kept warm

RED CURRY PASTE

1 tbsp coriander seeds

2 tsp cumin seeds

2 tsp black or white peppercorns

1 tsp salt, or to taste

5–8 dried hot red chillies

3–4 shallots, chopped

6–8 garlic cloves

5 cm/2 inch piece fresh galangal or ginger root, peeled and coarsely chopped

2 tsp kaffir lime rind or 2 fresh lime leaves, chopped

1 tbsp ground red chilli powder

1 tbsp shrimp paste

2 stalks lemon grass, thinly sliced

1 To make the red curry paste, grind the coriander seeds, cumin seeds, peppercorns and salt to a fine powder. Add the chillies, one by one, according to taste, until ground.

2 Put the shallots, garlic, galangal, kaffir lime rind, chilli powder and shrimp paste in a food processor. Process for about 1 minute.

3 Put about half the red curry paste in a large deep heavy-based frying pan with the pork. Cook over a medium heat for

Add the ground spices and process again. Adding water, a few drops at a time, continue to process until a thick paste forms. Scrape into a bowl and stir in the lemon grass.

2–3 minutes, stirring gently, until the pork is evenly coated and begins to brown.

4 Stir in the coconut milk and bring to the boil. Cook, stirring frequently, for about 10 minutes. Reduce the heat, stir in the chillies, Thai fish sauce and brown sugar and simmer for about 20 minutes. Add the red pepper and simmer for a further 10 minutes.

5 Add the lime leaves and half the mint and basil to the curry. Transfer to a serving dish, sprinkle with the remaining mint and basil and serve with the rice.

Mee Krob

Serves 4–6

INGREDIENTS

vegetable oil, for frying

350 g/12 oz fine rice vermicelli
noodles, unsoaked

4 eggs, lightly beaten

85 g/3 oz boned lean leg of pork,
thinly sliced

85 g/3 oz boned chicken breast,
skinned and thinly sliced

85 g/3 oz small peeled prawns

4–6 spring onions, thinly sliced on
the diagonal

3–4 fresh red chillies, thinly sliced
on the diagonal

4 tbsp rice vinegar

4 tbsp light soy sauce

4 tbsp Thai fish sauce

4–6 tbsp chicken stock or water

4 tbsp sugar

1 tsp coriander seeds, lightly
crushed

4 tbsp chopped fresh coriander

1 Heat at least 7.5 cm/
3 inches of vegetable oil
in a deep-fat fryer or wok to
180–190°C/350–375°F or
until a cube of bread browns
in 30 seconds.

2 Gently separate the layers
of noodles, then carefully
fry, one layer at a time, for
10–15 seconds until golden.
Transfer to kitchen paper to
drain; set aside.

3 Heat 1–2 tablespoons of
the hot oil in a large non-
stick frying pan. Pour in the

beaten egg to form a thin
layer and cook for about 1
minute until just set. Turn
and cook for 5 seconds
longer. Slide out of the pan
and cool slightly. Cut in half
and roll up each half, then
slice into 5mm/ ¼ inch strips.
Set aside.

4 Heat 2 more tablespoons
of the oil in a wok or
large, deep frying pan over a
medium-high heat. Add the
pork and chicken slices and
stir-fry for about 2 minutes,
or until cooked.

5 Add the prawns,
spring onions and
chillies and stir to mix. Push
the meat and vegetables to
one side. Add the vinegar,
soy sauce, fish sauce, stock,
sugar and coriander seeds to
the space in the pan, bubble
gently, then stir into the
meat mixture. Stir in the
omelette and half the fresh
coriander.

6 Add the warm noodles,
turn gently and sprinkle
with the remaining
coriander.

Nasi Goreng

Serves 4

INGREDIENTS

1 large onion, chopped

2–3 garlic cloves

1 tsp shrimp paste

2 red chillies, deseeded and chopped

125 ml/4 fl oz vegetable oil

3 eggs, lightly beaten

450 g/1 lb beef rump steak, about 1 cm/½ inch thick

2 carrots, cut into matchsticks

175 g/6 oz Chinese long beans or green beans, cut into 2.5cm/1 inch pieces

6 small spring onions, cut into 1 cm/½ inch pieces

250 g/9 oz raw shelled prawns

750 g/1 lb 10 oz cooked long-grain white rice, at room temperature

6 tbsp dark soy sauce

50 ml/2 fl oz water

TO GARNISH

4 tbsp ready-fried onion flakes

10 cm/4 inch piece cucumber, deseeded and cut into thin sticks

2 tbsp chopped fresh coriander

1 Put the onion, garlic, shrimp paste and chillies into a food processor and process until a paste forms. Add a little oil and process until smooth. Set aside.

2 Heat 1–2 tablespoons oil in a large, non-stick frying pan. Pour in the egg to form a thin layer and cook for 1 minute until just set. Turn and cook for 5 seconds on the other side. Slide out and cut in half. Roll up each

half, then slice into 5 mm/¼ inch wide strips. Set aside.

3 Heat 2 tablespoons oil in the same pan over a high heat and add the steak. Cook for 2 minutes on each side to brown and seal, but do not cook completely. Let cool, then cut into thin strips and reserve.

4 Heat 2 tablespoons oil in a large wok over a medium-high heat. Add the

reserved chilli paste and cook, stirring frequently, for about 3 minutes. Add 2 tablespoons of oil, the carrots and long beans. Stir-fry for about 2 minutes. Add the spring onions, prawns and the beef strips and stir-fry until the prawns are pink.

5 Stir in the rice, half the sliced omelette, 2 tablespoons soy sauce and 50 ml/2 fl oz water. Cover and steam for 1 minute. Spoon into a serving dish, top with the remaining omelette and drizzle with the remaining soy sauce. Sprinkle with a selection of the garnishes and serve.

Iranian Steamed Crusty Rice

Serves 6

INGREDIENTS

425 g/15 oz plus 1 tbsp basmati
   or long-grain white rice
salt

4 tbsp butter or ghee
50 ml/2 fl oz water

1 Bring at least 2 litres/ 3½ pints of water to the boil. Add 2 tablespoons of salt. Gradually add the ice, then simmer for 7–10 minutes until almost tender; stir gently occasionally. Drain and rinse under warm running water to remove any starch.

2 Heat the butter or ghee with the water in a large heavy-based saucepan over a medium-high heat until the butter melts and the water is steaming; remove half of this mixture and reserve. Spoon enough rice into the pan to cover the bottom, smoothing lightly and evenly.

3 Spoon the remaining rice into the pan. Cover the rice with a thin tea towel, then cover the pan tightly and reduce the heat to very low. Cook for 15 minutes.

4 Remove the covers and, with the handle of a wooden spoon, gently poke several holes into the rice to let the steam escape.

5 Pour the remaining butter-water mixture over the rice, re-cover as before and cook for a further 10–15 minutes. Uncover and transfer the pan to a chilled surface (see Cook's Tip); this helps to loosen the crust

from the bottom of the pan.

6 Using a fork, fluff the loose rice into a serving bowl. Break up the crusty brown layer into pieces and arrange around the serving dish. Traditionally, the honoured guest got the crusty layer!

COOK'S TIP

To chill the work surface for cooling down the saucepan of hot rice, place 2 ice-cube trays on the work surface ahead of time.

Chinese Fried Rice

Serves 4–6

INGREDIENTS

2–3 tbsp groundnut or
    vegetable oil
2 onions, halved and cut
    lengthways into thin wedges
2 garlic cloves, thinly sliced
2.5 cm/1 inch piece fresh ginger
    root, peeled, sliced and cut
    into slivers
200 g/7 oz cooked ham,

thinly sliced
750 g/1 lb 10 oz cooked, cold
    long-grain white rice
250 g/9 oz cooked peeled prawns
2 tbsp water
115 g/4 oz canned water
    chestnuts, sliced
3 eggs
3 tsp sesame oil

4–6 spring onions, diagonally
    sliced into 2.5 cm/1 inch
    pieces
2 tbsp dark soy sauce or Thai
    fish sauce
1 tbsp sweet chilli sauce
2 tbsp chopped fresh coriander
    or flat-leaved parsley
salt and pepper

1 Heat 2–3 tablespoons groundnut oil in a wok or large, deep frying pan until very hot. Add the onions and stir-fry for about 2 minutes until beginning to soften. Add the garlic and ginger and stir-fry for another minute. Add the ham strips and stir to combine.

2 Add the cold cooked rice and stir to mix with the vegetables and ham. Stir in the prawns and the water chestnuts. Stir in the water and cover the pan quickly. Continue to cook for 2 minutes, shaking the pan occasionally to prevent sticking and to let the rice heat through.

3 Beat the eggs with 1 teaspoon of the sesame oil and season with salt and pepper. Make a well in the centre of the rice mixture, add the eggs and immediately stir, gradually drawing the rice into the eggs.

4 Stir in the spring onions, soy sauce and chilli sauce and stir-fry; stir in a little more water if the rice looks dry or is sticking. Drizzle in the remaining sesame oil and stir. Season to taste with salt and pepper.

5 Remove from the heat, wipe the edge of the wok or frying pan and sprinkle with the coriander. Serve immediately from the pan.

Malayan Rice Noodle Soup

Serves 4–6

INGREDIENTS

1.25 kg/2 lb 12 oz corn-fed or free-range chicken
1 tsp black peppercorns
2 tbsp groundnut or vegetable oil
2 onions, thinly sliced
2–3 garlic cloves, minced
5 cm/1 inch piece fresh ginger root, peeled and thinly sliced
1 tsp ground coriander

2 fresh red chillies, deseeded and thinly sliced on the diagonal
½–1 tsp ground turmeric
½ tsp Madras curry paste
400 ml/14 fl oz canned coconut milk
450 g/1 lb large raw prawns, peeled and de-veined
½ small head of Chinese leaves, thinly shredded

1 tsp sugar
2 spring onions, thinly sliced
115 g/4 oz beansprouts
250 g/9 oz rice noodles, rice vermicelli or rice sticks, soaked according to packet instructions
handful of fresh mint leaves, to garnish

1 Stock: Put the chicken in a large pan with the peppercorns and enough cold water just to cover. Bring to the boil, then simmer for 1 hour, skimming off any foam.

2 Remove the chicken; cool. Skim any fat from the liquid and strain through muslin; set aside. Remove the meat from the carcass; shred.

3 Heat the oil in a deep frying pan until very hot. Add the onions to the pan and stir-fry for about 2 minutes until they begin to colour. Stir in the garlic, ginger, coriander, chillies, turmeric and curry paste. Transfer to a large pan and slowly stir in the stock. Simmer, partially covered, over low heat for about 20 minutes or until the stock has slightly reduced.

4 Add the coconut milk, prawns, Chinese leaves, sugar, spring onions and beansprouts to the simmering

COOK'S TIP

Corn-fed chickens are reared on a diet of sweetcorn, which gives them a yellow colour and delicious flavour.

stock, cook for about 3 minutes, stirring occasionally, until the prawns are pink. Add the shredded chicken and cook for 2 minutes.

5 Drain the noodles and divide between 4–6 bowls. Ladle on the hot stock and vegetables. Make sure each serving has some of the prawns and the shredded chicken. Garnish with mint leaves. Serve immediately.

Singapore Noodles

Serves 4–6

INGREDIENTS

60 g/2¼ oz dried Chinese
mushrooms

225 g/8 oz rice vermicelli
noodles

2–3 tbsp groundnut or
vegetable oil

6–8 garlic cloves, thinly sliced

2–3 shallots, thinly sliced

2.5 cm/1 inch piece fresh ginger
root, peeled and thinly sliced

4–5 fresh red chillies, deseeded
and thinly sliced on the
diagonal

225 g/8 oz boned chicken
breasts, skinned and
thinly sliced

225 g/8 oz mangetout, thinly
sliced on the diagonal

225 g/8 oz Chinese leaves,
thinly shredded

225 g/8 oz cooked peeled
prawns

6–8 water chestnuts, sliced

2 spring onions, thinly sliced on
the diagonal

2 tbsp chopped fresh coriander
or mint

SINGAPORE CURRY SAUCE

2 tbsp rice wine or dry sherry

2 tbsp soy sauce

3 tbsp medium or hot Madras
curry powder

1 tbsp sugar

400 ml/14 fl oz canned
coconut milk

1 tsp salt

4–5 grinds black pepper

1 To make the curry sauce, whisk the rice wine and soy sauce into the curry powder, then stir in the remaining ingredients.

2 Put the Chinese mushrooms in a small bowl and add enough boiling water to cover. Leave for about 15 minutes until softened. Lift out and

squeeze out the liquid. Discard any stems, then slice thinly and set aside. Soak the rice noodles according to the instructions on the packet, then drain well.

3 Heat the oil in a wok or deep frying pan over a medium-high heat. Add the garlic, shallots, ginger and chillies and stir-fry for about

30 seconds. Add the chicken and mangetout and stir-fry for about 2 minutes. Add the Chinese leaves, prawns, water chestnuts, mushrooms and spring onions and stir-fry for 1–2 minutes. Add the curry sauce and noodles; stir-fry for 5 minutes. Add the coriander; serve.

Vietnamese Spring Rolls

Makes 25–30 rolls

INGREDIENTS

25–30 rice paper wrappers
4–5 tbsp plain flour, mixed to a
    paste with 4–5 tbsp water
vegetable oil, for frying
sliced spring onions, to garnish

FILLING
15 g/½ oz dried Chinese
    mushrooms

1–2 tbsp groundnut or
    vegetable oil
1 small onion, finely chopped
3–4 garlic cloves
4 cm/1½ inch piece fresh ginger
    root, peeled and chopped
225 g/8 oz minced pork
2 spring onions, finely chopped
115 g/4 oz fresh beansprouts
4 water chestnuts, chopped

2 tbsp fresh chives, thinly sliced
175 g/6 oz small cooked peeled
    prawns, roughly chopped
1 tsp oyster sauce
1 tsp light soy sauce
60 g/2¼ oz rice vermicelli or
    cellophane noodles, soaked
    according to packet
    instructions
salt and pepper

1 To make the filling, cover the Chinese mushrooms with boiling water. Stand for about 15 minutes until softened and squeeze out the liquid. Discard any stems and slice thinly.

2 Heat the oil in a wok over high heat. Add the onion, garlic and ginger and stir-fry for 2 minutes. Add the pork and soaked mushrooms and stir-fry for about 4 minutes until the

pork is cooked and any liquid evaporates. Stir in the spring onions. Transfer to a bowl; cool.

3 Stir in the beansprouts, water chestnuts, chives and prawns with the oyster and soy sauces. Season with salt and pepper. Add the noodles and toss.

4 To assemble the spring rolls, soften a rice paper wrapper in warm water for a

few seconds, then drain on a clean dry tea towel. Put 2 tablespoons of the filling near one edge of the wrapper, fold the edge over the filling to cover, then fold in each side and roll up. Seal with a little of the flour paste; set aside. Make the remaining rolls.

5 Heat about 10 cm/ 4 inches of oil in a deep-fat fryer to 180–190°C/ 350–375°F or until a cube of bread browns in 30 seconds. Fry the spring rolls a few at a time for about 2 minutes, turning once or twice, until golden. Drain on kitchen paper, then serve garnished with spring onion.

Japanese Sushi

Serves 4–6

INGREDIENTS

475 ml/17 fl oz water
400 g/14 oz sushi rice
4 tbsp Japanese rice vinegar
1½ tbsp caster sugar
1½ tsp salt
1½ tbsp mirin (Japanese
    rice wine)

NORIMAKI SUSHI
2 eggs
pinch of turmeric
1–2 tbsp vegetable oil
4 sheets dried nori seaweed
115 g/4 oz smoked salmon slices,
    cut into 7.5 cm/3 inch pieces
½ cucumber, lightly peeled,
    quartered, deseeded, then
    thinly sliced lengthways
fresh chives

NIGIRI SUSHI
16 cooked peeled prawns
wasabi paste (Japanese
    horseradish)
85 g/3 oz smoked salmon fillet,
    cut into 5 mm/¼ inch slices
sesame seeds, lightly toasted

TO SERVE
pickled ginger
Japanese soy sauce

1 Bring the water and the rice to the boil, then simmer, covered, for 20 minutes until just tender. Stand for 10 minutes, covered.

2 Bring to the boil the vinegar, sugar, salt and mirin. Pour the vinegar mixture evenly over the surface of the rice. Quickly blend into the rice, fanning the rice at the same time as it cools.

3 For the norimaki sushi, beat the eggs with the turmeric and 1 teaspoon of the oil, then use to make 2 omelettes, cooking in the remaining oil. Cut in half.

4 Pass the sheets of nori over a flame for a few minutes to toast. Lay a piece of nori, toasted-side down, on a bamboo sushi mat. Lay an omelette half on top, leaving a border around the edge. Spread

a thin layer of sushi rice over. Place a piece of smoked salmon on the bottom third of the rice, trimming to fit, and top with cucumber and a few chives.

5 Moisten the border of the nori with a little water and, using the mat as a guide, roll up. Do the rest and leave to set, seam-side down. Cut into 2.5 cm/1 inch slices, cover and chill.

6 For the nigiri sushi, using wet hands, shape 2 tablespoons of the rice at a time into oblongs or ovals. Top with 2 prawns, or a dab of wasabi and some smoked salmon. Sprinkle with the toasted sesame seeds. Serve the sushi with the pickled ginger and Japanese soy sauce.

Puddings,
Cakes & Pastries

One of the best ways to use rice is in desserts. Its delicate flavour and starchy characteristics are ideal for many puddings, cakes and sweets. Who can resist Meringue-Topped Rice Pudding, a thick creamy vanilla-scented rice topped with a sweet golden meringue – the perfect dessert for a cold winter night?

Every nationality seems to have developed a rice pudding, from the grand moulded Riz à l'Impératrice of France, to the classic Indian rice pudding, Kesari Kheer, which is tinted a stunning yellow with saffron. Sometimes only ground rice or rice flour is cooked with milk until it thickens into a rich creamy dish, like the Lebanese Almond Rice Pudding – absolutely delicious.

Rice gives texture to cakes like the Italian Lemon Rice Cake, a divine creation flavoured with rum and dried fruit, and the Rice Muffins, delicious with amaretti butter. An Italian ice cream is given an interesting twist with the addition of rice, while Spicy Carrot-rice Cake is a variation on an old favourite. Rice flour replaces a little flour in baked goods like Scottish Shortbread and Persian Rice Crescents, where it lends a fine texture and delicate flavour.

Meringue-topped Rice Pudding

Serves 6–8

INGREDIENTS

125 ml/4 fl oz water
1.2 litres/2 pints milk
100 g/3½ oz long-grain
　white rice
2–3 strips of lemon rind

1 cinnamon stick
1 vanilla pod, split
115 g/4 oz sugar
3 tbsp cornflour
4 egg yolks

MERINGUE
6 egg whites
¼ tsp cream of tartar
225 g/8 oz caster sugar

1 Bring the water and 225 ml/8 fl oz of the milk to the boil in a large heavy-based saucepan. Add the rice, lemon rind, cinnamon stick and vanilla pod and reduce the heat to low. Cover and simmer for about 20 minutes until the rice is tender and all the liquid is absorbed. Remove the lemon rind, cinnamon stick and vanilla pod and add the remaining milk; return to the boil.

2 Stir together the sugar and the cornflour. Stir in a little of the hot rice-milk to make a paste, then stir into

the pan of rice. Cook, stirring constantly, until the mixture boils and thickens. Boil for 1 minute, then remove from the heat to cool slightly.

3 Beat the egg yolks until smooth. Stir a large spoonful of the hot rice mixture into the yolks, beating until well blended, then stir into the rice mixture. Pour into a 3 litre/ 5¼ pint baking dish.

4 To make the meringue, beat the egg whites with the cream of tartar in a large bowl to form stiff peaks. Add

the sugar, 2 tablespoons at a time, beating well after each addition, until stiff and glossy.

5 Gently spoon the meringue over the top of the rice pudding, spreading evenly. Make swirls with the back of the spoon.

6 Bake in a preheated oven at 150°C/300°F/Gas Mark 2 for about 1 hour until the top is golden and set. Turn off the oven, open the door and let the pudding cool in the oven. Serve warm, at room temperature, or cold.

Basmati Pudding with Bay & Orange

Serves 4

INGREDIENTS

600 ml/1 pint milk
225 m/8 fl oz single cream
4 fresh bay leaves, washed and
gently bruised

4 tbsp basmati or long-grain
white rice
60 g/2¼ oz sugar
2 tbsp sultanas or raisins
grated rind of 1 orange

1 tsp vanilla essence
2 tbsp pine kernels or
green pistachios
fancy biscuits, to serve

1 Put the milk and cream in a medium heavy-based saucepan and bring to the boil over a medium heat, stirring occasionally to prevent sticking.

2 Add the bay leaves, then sprinkle in the rice. Reduce the heat to low and simmer gently for about 1 hour, stirring occasionally, until the rice is tender and the mixture is thickened and creamy.

3 Stir in the sugar, sultanas and orange rind and stir frequently until the sugar is dissolved and the fruit is plump. Remove from the heat, discard the bay leaves and stir in the vanilla.

4 Meanwhile, toast the pine kernels in a small frying pan until golden.

5 Spoon the pudding into individual bowls and sprinkle with the toasted nuts.

Serve warm, or refrigerate to thicken and chill. Hand round the biscuits separately.

VARIATION

Bay has a lovely flavour and goes well with rice, but, if preferred, you can substitute a cinnamon stick, lightly crushed cardamom seeds, freshly grated nutmeg or seeds from a vanilla pod.

Raspberry Risotto with Glazed Raspberries

Serves 4–6

INGREDIENTS

450 ml/16 fl oz milk
450 ml/16 fl oz canned
    unsweetened coconut milk
pinch of salt
1 vanilla pod, split
2–3 strips lemon rind
2 tbsp unsalted butter

125 g/4¹/₂ oz arborio rice
50 ml/2 fl oz dry white vermouth
100 g/3¹/₂ oz sugar
125 ml/4 fl oz double or
    whipping cream
2–3 tbsp raspberry-flavoured
    liqueur

350 g/12 oz fresh raspberries
2 tbsp good-quality raspberry
    jam or preserve
squeeze of lemon juice
toasted flaked almonds,
    to decorate (optional)

1 Heat the milk in a heavy-based saucepan with the coconut milk, salt, vanilla pod and lemon rind until bubbles begin to form around the edge of the pan. Reduce the heat to low and keep the milk mixture hot, stirring occasionally.

2 Heat the butter in another large heavy-based pan over a medium heat until foaming. Add the rice and cook, stirring, for 2 minutes to coat well.

3 Add the vermouth; it will bubble and steam rapidly. Cook, stirring, until the wine is completely absorbed. Gradually add the hot milk, about 125 ml/4 fl oz at a time, allowing each addition to be absorbed completely before adding the next.

4 When half the milk has been added, stir in the sugar until dissolved. Continue stirring and adding the milk until the rice is tender, but still firm to the bite: this should take

about 25 minutes. Remove from the heat; remove the vanilla pod and lemon strips. Stir in half the cream, the liqueur and half the fresh raspberries; cover.

5 Heat the raspberry jam with the lemon juice and 1–2 tablespoons water, stirring until smooth. Remove from heat, add the remaining raspberries and mix. Stir the remaining cream into the risotto and serve with the glazed raspberries. Decorate if wished.

Snowdon Pudding

Serves 4

INGREDIENTS

butter, for greasing	125 g/4½ oz shredded suet	LEMON SAUCE
115 g/4 oz raisins	2 tbsp light brown sugar	1 tbsp cornflour
2 tbsp chopped angelica	grated rind of 1 large lemon	250 ml/9 fl oz milk
115 g/4 oz fresh white	2 eggs	grated rind and juice of 2 lemons
breadcrumbs	85 g/3 oz marmalade	3 tbsp golden syrup
25 g/1 oz rice flour	3–4 tsp milk	
pinch of salt		

1 Sprinkle a well-buttered 1.2 litre/2 pint pudding basin with a tablespoon of the raisins and the angelica.

2 Put the remaining raisins in a bowl with the breadcrumbs, rice flour, salt, suet, sugar and lemon rind and toss to combine. Make a well in the centre.

3 Beat the eggs and marmalade for about 1 minute until beginning to lighten. Beat in 3 tablespoons of the milk; pour into the well. Gently stir into the dry ingredients to form a soft dough. Add more milk if necessary. Spoon into the prepared pudding basin.

4 Butter a sheet of baking parchment and make a pleat along the centre. Cover the basin loosely with the paper, buttered-side down; secure with string.

5 Stand the pudding basin on a wire rack in a large pan. Fill with enough boiling water to come three quarters of the way up the side of the basin. Cover and steam gently over low heat for about 2 hours until the top is risen. Top up with boiling water when needed.

6 To make the lemon sauce, mix the cornflour with about 3 tablespoons of milk to form a paste. Bring the remaining milk and the lemon rind to the simmer, then whisk into the paste until blended. Return the mixture to the pan and simmer gently for about 3 minutes, whisking, until smooth. Stir in the lemon juice and syrup. Pour into a jug; keep warm.

7 Remove the pudding from the pan, remove the paper and let the pudding shrink slightly before unmoulding. Serve hot with the lemon sauce.

Florentine Rice Pudding

Serves 6

INGREDIENTS

150 g/5½ oz long-grain white
   rice or Italian arborio rice
pinch of salt
1 litre/1¾ pints milk
5 eggs
400 g/14 oz sugar or 450 g/

1 lb honey, or a mixture
115 g/4 oz butter, melted
   and cooled
2 tbsp orange flower water or
   4 tbsp orange-flavoured
   liqueur

225 g/8 oz diced candied
   orange peel
225 g/8 oz orange marmalade
2–3 tablespoons water
icing sugar, for dusting

1 Put the rice and salt in a large heavy-bottomed saucepan. Add the milk and bring to the boil, stirring occasionally. Reduce the heat to low and simmer gently for about 25 minutes until the rice is tender and creamy. Remove from the heat.

2 Pass the cooked rice through a food mill into a large bowl. Alternatively, process in a food processor for about 30 seconds until smooth. Set aside. Stir from time to time to prevent a skin forming.

3 Meanwhile, using an electric mixer, beat the eggs with the sugar in a large bowl for about 4 minutes until very light and creamy. Gently fold into the rice with the melted butter. Stir in half the orange flower water, then stir in the candied orange peel.

4 Turn into a well-buttered 2 litre/3½ pint soufflé dish or charlotte mould. Place the dish in a roasting tin and pour in enough boiling water to come 4 cm/ 1½ inches up the side of the dish.

5 Bake in a preheated oven at 180°C/350°F/ Gas Mark 4 for about 25 minutes until puffed and lightly set. Transfer the dish to a wire rack to cool slightly.

6 Heat the marmalade with the water, stirring until dissolved and smooth. Stir in the remaining orange flower water and pour into a sauceboat. Dust the top of the pudding with the icing sugar and serve warm with the marmalade sauce.

Almond Rice Custard

Serves 6

INGREDIENTS

85 g/3 oz whole blanched
    almonds
1 litre/1¾ pints milk
25 g/1 oz rice flour
pinch of salt

60 g/2¼ oz sugar
½ tsp almond essence or 1 tbsp
    almond-flavour liqueur
toasted flaked almonds,
    to decorate

TO SERVE (OPTIONAL)
350 g/12 oz fresh strawberries,
    sliced, sprinkled with 2 tbsp
    sugar and chilled

1 Put the almonds in a food processor and process until a thick paste forms. Bring 225 ml/8 fl oz of the milk to the boil. Gradually pour into the almond paste, with the machine running, until the mixture is smooth. Leave to stand for about 10 minutes.

2 Combine the rice flour, salt and sugar in a large bowl, then stir in about 4–5 tablespoons of the milk to form a smooth paste.

3 Bring the remaining milk to the boil in a heavy-based saucepan. Pour the hot milk into the rice flour paste and stir constantly, then return the mixture to the saucepan and bring to the boil. Reduce the heat and simmer for about 10 minutes until smooth and thickened. Remove from the heat.

4 Strain the almond milk through a very fine sieve into the simmering rice custard, pressing through the

almonds with the back of a spoon. Return to the heat and simmer for a further 7–10 minutes or until it becomes thick.

5 Remove from the heat and stir in the almond essence. Cool slightly, stirring, then pour into individual bowls. Sprinkle with the almonds and serve with the strawberries, if wished. Chill to serve later, if preferred – the custard will thicken as it cools.

Black Rice Pudding with Mango Salad

Serves 6–8

INGREDIENTS

300 g/10½ oz black
   glutinous rice
850 ml/1½ pints boiling water
1 vanilla pod, split, black seeds
   removed and reserved
225 g/8 oz light
   brown sugar

55 g/2 oz packet coconut
   powder
400 ml/14 fl oz can thick
   coconut milk
2 ripe mangoes
6 passion fruit

TO DECORATE
shredded fresh coconut
   (optional)
fresh mint leaves, to decorate

1 Put the rice in a large heavy-based saucepan and pour over the boiling water. Add the vanilla pod and seeds to the pan. Return to the boil, stirring once or twice. Reduce the heat to low and simmer, covered, for about 25 minutes until the rice is tender and the liquid almost absorbed; do not uncover during cooking.

2 Remove from the heat and stir in the sugar, coconut powder and half the coconut milk. Stir until the sugar is dissolved. Cover and stand for 10 minutes. If the rice becomes too thick, add a little more of the coconut milk or a little milk or water.

3 Cut each mango lengthways along each side of the large stone to remove the flesh. Peel the mangoes, thinly slice and arrange on a serving plate.

4 Cut the passion fruit crossways in half and scoop out the pulp and juice; spoon over the mango slices. Decorate with shredded coconut, if wished, and a few mint leaves.

5 Spoon the warm pudding into wide shallow bowls and decorate with shredded coconut and mint leaves. Drizzle some of the remaining coconut milk around the edges, if wished. Serve with the mango salad.

Rice Pudding Tartlets

Makes 6–8 tartlets

INGREDIENTS

1 quantity Shortcrust Pastry
(see page 150)
1 litre/1¾ pints milk
pinch of salt
100 g/3½ oz arborio or
long-grain white rice

1 vanilla pod, split, seeds
removed and reserved
1 tbsp cornflour
2 tbsp sugar
cocoa powder, to dust
melted chocolate, to decorate

CHOCOLATE GANACHE
200 ml/7 fl oz double cream
1 tbsp golden syrup
175 g/6 oz plain or continental
plain chocolate, chopped
1 tbsp unsalted butter

1 Make the pastry shells following Steps 1–4 on page 150, increasing the sugar to 2 tablespoons. After removing the beans in Step 4, bake for 5–7 minutes longer until the pastry is crisp. Transfer the tartlets to a wire rack to cool.

2 To make the chocolate ganache, bring the double cream and golden syrup to the boil. Remove from the heat and immediately stir in the chopped chocolate; stir until melted and smooth. Beat in the butter. Spoon a 2.5 cm/1 inch thick layer into each tartlet. Set aside.

3 Bring the milk and salt to the boil in a saucepan. Sprinkle in the rice and return to the boil. Add the vanilla seeds and pod. Reduce the heat and simmer until the rice is tender and the milk creamy.

4 Blend the cornflour and sugar in a small bowl and add about 2 tablespoons water to make a paste. Stir in a few spoonfuls of the rice mixture, then stir the cornflour mixture into the rice. Bring to the boil and cook for about 1 minute until thickened. Cool the pan in iced water, stirring until thick.

5 Spoon into the tartlets, filling each to the brim. Leave to set at room temperature. To serve, dust with cocoa powder and pipe or drizzle with melted chocolate.

Riz à l'Impératrice

Serves 6–8

INGREDIENTS

125 ml/4 fl oz kirsch or other
favourite liqueur
115 g/4 oz candied or dried fruits,
such as dried sour cherries,
dried cranberries or
blueberries, raisins or
candied peel
100 g/3½ oz long-grain

white rice
pinch of salt
700 ml/1¼ pints milk
60 g/2¼ oz caster sugar
1 vanilla pod, split open, seeds
scraped out and reserved
1 sachet unflavoured powdered
gelatine

50 ml/2 fl oz cold water
2 egg yolks, lightly beaten
225 ml/8 fl oz double cream,
whipped until soft peaks
form
4 tbsp apricot jam or preserve
glacé cherries, to decorate

1 Combine 2–3 tablespoons of the kirsch with the candied or dried fruits and set aside.

2 Bring a saucepan of water to the boil. Sprinkle in the rice and add the salt; simmer gently for 15–20 minutes until the rice is just tender. Drain, rinse and drain again.

3 Bring the milk and sugar to the boil in a large non-stick saucepan. Add the vanilla seeds and pod and stir in the rice. Reduce the heat to low and simmer, covered, until the rice is very tender and the milk reduced by about a third. Remove from the heat and discard the vanilla pod.

4 Soften the gelatine in the water, then heat gently to dissolve.

5 Add about 2 tablespoons of the hot rice to the egg yolks and whisk to blend, then beat into the rice with the dissolved gelatine until the mixture thickens slightly. Pour into a large mixing bowl.

Place the bowl in a roasting tin half-filled with iced water and stir until beginning to set.

6 Fold in the soaked fruits and cream. Stir until it begins to set again, then immediately pour into a rinsed 1.2–1.5 litre/2–2¾ pint mould. Smooth the surface, cover and chill for at least 2 hours or overnight.

7 Unmould the rice on to a serving plate. Heat the jam with the remaining kirsch and 2 tablespoons water to make a smooth glaze. Brush over the top of the unmoulded rice. Decorate the dessert with cherries and stand for 15 minutes before serving.

Chocolate Rice Dessert

Serves 8–10

INGREDIENTS

100 g/3½ oz long-grain
    white rice
pinch of salt
600 ml/1 pint milk
100 g/3½ oz sugar

200 g/7 oz plain or continental
    plain chocolate, chopped
4 tbsp butter, diced
1 tsp vanilla essence
2 tbsp brandy or Cognac

175 ml/6 fl oz double cream
whipped cream, for piping
    (optional)
chocolate curls, to decorate
    (optional)

1 Bring a saucepan of water to the boil. Sprinkle in the rice and add the salt; reduce the heat and simmer gently for 15–20 minutes until the rice is just tender. Drain, rinse and drain again.

2 Heat the milk and the sugar in a large heavy-based saucepan over a medium heat until the sugar dissolves, stirring frequently. Add the chocolate and butter and stir until melted and smooth.

3 Stir in the cooked rice and reduce the heat to low. Cover and simmer, stirring occasionally, for 30 minutes until the milk is absorbed and the mixture thickened. Stir in the vanilla extract and brandy. Remove from the heat and let cool to room temperature.

4 Using an electric mixer, beat the cream until soft peaks form. Stir one heaped spoonful of the cream into the chocolate rice mixture to lighten it; then fold in the remaining cream.

5 Spoon into glass serving dishes, cover and chill for about 2 hours. If wished, decorate with piped whipped cream and top with chocolate curls. Serve cold.

VARIATION

To mould the chocolate rice, soften 1 sachet gelatine in about 50 ml/2 fl oz cold water and heat gently until dissolved. Stir into the chocolate just before folding in the cream. Pour into a rinsed mould, let it set, then unmould.

Orange-scented Rice Pudding

Serves 6

INGREDIENTS

140 g/5 oz pudding rice
225 ml/8 fl oz freshly squeezed
orange juice
pinch of salt
500 ml/18 fl oz milk
1 vanilla pod, split

5 cm/2 inch piece fresh ginger
root, peeled and gently
bruised
200 g/7 oz sugar
50 ml/2 fl oz double cream
4 tbsp orange-flavoured liqueur

2 tbsp butter
4–6 seedless oranges
2 pieces stem ginger, sliced
thinly, plus 2 tbsp ginger
syrup from the jar
ground ginger, for dusting

1 Put the rice in a large heavy-based saucepan with the orange juice and salt. Bring to the boil, skimming off any foam. Reduce the heat to low and simmer gently for 10 minutes, stirring occasionally, until the juice is absorbed.

2 Gradually stir in the milk, add the vanilla pod and ginger root and continue to simmer for about 30 minutes, stirring frequently, until the milk is absorbed and the rice is very tender. Remove from the

heat; remove the vanilla pod and ginger root.

3 Stir in half the sugar, half the cream, the orange liqueur and the butter until the sugar is dissolved and the butter is melted. Let cool, stir in the remaining cream and pour into a serving bowl. Leave at room temperature.

4 Pare the rind from the oranges and reserve. Working over a bowl to catch the juices, remove the pith from all the oranges. Cut out the segments and drop into

the bowl. Stir in the stem ginger and syrup. Chill.

5 Cut the pared orange rind into thin strips and blanch for 1 minute. Drain and rinse. Bring 225 ml/ 8 fl oz/1 cup of water to the boil with the remaining sugar. Add the rind strips and simmer gently until the syrup is reduced by half. Cool.

6 Serve the pudding with the chilled oranges, top with the caramelized orange rind strips, and dust with the ground ginger.

Kesari Kheer

Serves 4–6

INGREDIENTS

2 tbsp clarified butter or ghee

85 g/3 oz basmati rice, washed and well drained

1.5 litres/2¾ pints milk

115 g/4 oz sugar or to taste

10–12 green cardamom pods, crushed to remove the black

seeds (pods discarded)

70 g/2½ oz sultanas or raisins

large pinch saffron threads, about ½ tsp, soaked in 2–3 tbsp milk

60 g/2¼ oz green pistachios, lightly toasted

150 ml/5 fl oz double cream, whipped (optional)

ground cinnamon, for dusting

edible silver foil (vark), to decorate (optional)

1 Melt the butter in a large, heavy-based saucepan over a medium heat. Pour in the rice and cook, stirring almost constantly, for about 6 minutes until the rice grains are translucent and a deep golden brown.

2 Pour in the milk and over a high heat bring to the boil. Reduce the heat to medium-high and simmer for about 30 minutes, stirring occasionally, until the milk has reduced by about half.

3 Add the sugar, cardamom seeds and sultanas and cook for about 20 minutes until reduced and thick. Stir in the saffron-milk mixture and simmer over a low heat until as thick as possible, stirring almost constantly. Remove from the heat and stir in half the pistachios.

4 Place the saucepan in a larger pan of iced water and stir until cool. If using, stir in the cream, then spoon into a serving bowl and chill.

5 To serve, dust the top of the pudding with ground cinnamon. Sprinkle with the remaining pistachios and, if using, decorate with pieces of the silver foil (vark).

COOK'S TIP

The edible silver foil (vark) is available in some Asian or Indian supermarkets or speciality stores.

Lebanese Almond Rice Pudding

Serves 6

INGREDIENTS

40 g/1½ oz rice flour
pinch of salt
700 ml/1¼ pints milk
60 g/2¼ oz caster sugar
85 g/3 oz ground
    almonds
1 tbsp rosewater

TO DECORATE
2 tbsp chopped pistachios or
    toasted flaked almonds
pomegranate seeds (optional)
washed rose petals (optional)

1 Put the rice flour in a bowl, stir in the salt and make a well in the centre.

2 Pour in about 50 ml/ 2 fl oz of the milk and whisk to form a smooth paste.

3 Bring the remaining milk to the boil in a heavy-based saucepan. Whisk in the rice flour paste and the sugar and cook, stirring continuously, until the mixture thickens and bubbles. Reduce the heat and simmer gently for 5 minutes.

4 Whisk in the ground almonds until the pudding is smooth and thickened, then remove from the heat to cool slightly. Stir in the rosewater and cool completely, stirring occasionally.

5 Divide the mixture between 6 glasses or pour into a serving bowl. Chill for at least 2 hours before serving.

6 To serve, sprinkle with the pistachios or almonds and pomegranate seeds, if available. Scatter with rose petals, if wished.

COOK'S TIP

For a smoother texture, this can be made without the ground almonds. Stir 2 tablespoons of cornflour into the ground rice and use a little more of the milk to make the paste. Proceed as directed, omitting the ground almonds.

Portuguese Rice Pudding

Serves 6–8

INGREDIENTS

200 g/7 oz Spanish valencia,
    Italian arborio or pudding rice
pinch salt
1 lemon
450 ml/16 fl oz milk

150 ml/5 fl oz single
    cream
1 cinnamon stick
85 g/3 oz butter
140 g/5 oz sugar
    (or to taste)

8 egg yolks
ground cinnamon, for dusting
thick or double cream,
    to serve

1 Bring a saucepan of water to the boil. Sprinkle in the rice and salt and return to the boil; reduce the heat and simmer until just tender. Drain, rinse and drain.

2 Using a small sharp knife or swivel-bladed vegetable peeler, and working in a circular motion, try to peel the rind off the lemon in one curly piece; this makes it easier to remove later. Alternatively, peel off in strips.

3 Bring the milk and cream to a simmer over a medium heat. Add the rice, cinnamon stick, butter and the lemon rind 'curl' or strips. Reduce the heat to low and simmer gently for about 20 minutes until thick and creamy. Remove from the heat; remove and discard the cinnamon stick and the lemon rind. Stir in the sugar until dissolved.

4 In a large bowl, beat the egg yolks until well blended. Gradually beat in the rice mixture until thick and smooth. Continue to stir frequently to prevent the eggs from curdling, until slightly cooled, then pour into a bowl or 6–8 individual glasses. Dust with ground cinnamon and serve at room temperature, with cream.

Rice Pudding Brulée

Serves 6–8

INGREDIENTS

200 g/7 oz arborio rice
pinch of salt
1 vanilla pod, split
700 ml/1¼ pints milk

200 g/7 oz caster sugar
2 egg yolks
125 ml/4 fl oz double or
    whipping cream

grated rind of 1 large lemon
4 tbsp butter
2 tbsp brandy or Cognac
light brown sugar, for glazing

1 Put the rice in a large heavy-based saucepan with a pinch of salt and add enough cold water to just cover. Bring to the boil, then reduce the heat and simmer gently for about 12 minutes until the water is absorbed.

2 Scrape the seeds from the split vanilla pod into the milk. Bring to the simmer and pour over the rice. Add the sugar, and cook over a low heat, stirring, until the rice is tender and the milk thickened.

3 In a small bowl, beat the egg yolks with the cream and lemon rind. Stir in a large spoonful of the rice mixture and beat well to blend. Return the mixture to the pan and cook very gently until the pudding is thick and creamy; do not let it boil. Stir in the butter.

4 Remove from the heat and stir in the brandy; remove the vanilla pod. Carefully spoon the mixture into 6–8 flameproof ramekins or crème brûlée pots. Allow to cool, then chill for at least 2 hours.

5 Sprinkle a very thin layer of brown sugar on top of each ramekin, to cover completely. Wipe the edge of each ramekin as the sugar may stick and burn.

6 Place the ramekins in a small roasting tin filled with about 1 cm/½ inch iced water. Place under a preheated grill, close to the heat, and grill until the sugar melts and caramelizes. Alternatively, use a small blowtorch to caramelize the sugar.

7 Cool the ramekins for 2–3 minutes before serving.

Italian Rice Ice Cream

Makes about 1.2 litres/2 pints

INGREDIENTS

100 g/3 ½ oz short-grain
    pudding rice
500 ml/18 fl oz milk
85 g/3 oz sugar
85 g/3 oz good-quality honey

½ tsp lemon essence
1 tsp vanilla essence
175 g/6 oz good-quality
    lemon curd

500 ml/18 fl oz double or
    whipping cream
grated rind and juice of
    1 large lemon

1 Put the rice and milk in a large heavy-based saucepan and bring to a gentle simmer, stirring occasionally; do not let it boil. Reduce the heat to low, cover and simmer very gently for about 10 minutes, stirring occasionally, until the rice is just tender and the liquid absorbed.

2 Remove from the heat and stir in the sugar, honey and lemon and vanilla essences, stirring until the sugar is dissolved. Pour into a food processor and pulse 3 or 4 times. The mixture should be thick and creamy,

but it should not be completely smooth.

3 Put the lemon curd in a bowl and gradually beat in about 225 ml/8 fl oz of the cream. Stir in the rice mixture with the lemon rind and juice until blended. Lightly whip the remaining cream until it just begins to hold its shape, then fold into the lemon-rice mixture. Chill.

4 Stir the rice mixture and pour into an ice-cream machine. Churn according to the manufacturers' instructions

for 15–20 minutes. Transfer to a freezerproof container and freeze for 6–8 hours or overnight. Transfer to the refrigerator about 1 hour before serving.

COOK'S TIP

If you do not have an ice-cream machine, transfer the chilled rice mixture to a freezerproof container. Freeze for 1 hour until slightly slushy, then whisk to break up any crystals; refreeze. Repeat twice more.

Scottish Shortbread

Makes 16 wedges

INGREDIENTS

225 g/8 oz plain flour
60 g/2 oz rice flour
¼ tsp salt
175 g/6 oz unsalted butter, at
    room temperature

60 g/2¼ oz caster sugar
25 g/1 oz icing sugar, sifted
¼ tsp vanilla essence (optional)
sugar, for sprinkling

1 Lightly grease two 20–23 cm/8–9 inch cake or tart tins with removable bases. Sift the plain flour, rice flour and salt into a bowl; set aside.

2 Using an electric mixer, beat the butter for about 1 minute in a large bowl until creamy. Add the sugars and continue beating for 1–2 minutes until very light and fluffy. If using, beat in the vanilla.

3 Using a wooden spoon, stir the flour mixture into the butter and sugar until well blended. Turn on to a lightly floured surface and knead lightly to blend completely.

4 Divide the dough evenly between the 2 tins, smoothing the surface. Using a fork, press 2 cm/ ¾ inch radiating lines around the edge of the dough. Lightly sprinkle the surfaces with a little sugar, then prick the surface lightly with the fork.

5 Using a sharp knife, mark each dough round into 8 wedges. Bake in a preheated oven at 120°C/250°F/Gas Mark ½ for 50–60 minutes until pale golden and crisp. Cool in the tins on a wire rack for about 5 minutes.

6 Carefully remove the side of each pan and slide the bottoms on to a heatproof surface. Using the knife marks as a guide, cut each shortbread into 8 wedges while still warm. Cool completely on the wire rack, then store in airtight containers.

Persian Rice Crescents

Makes about 60 crescents

INGREDIENTS

225 g/8 oz unsalted butter,
  softened
115 g/4 oz icing sugar, sifted
2 egg yolks

½–1 tsp ground cardamom or
  1 tbsp rosewater
250 g/9 oz rice flour, sifted
1 egg white, lightly beaten

60 g/2¼ oz finely chopped
  pistachio nuts or almonds

1 Using an electric mixer, beat the butter until light and creamy in a large bowl for about 1 minute. On low speed, gradually add the icing sugar and beat for about 2 minutes until light and fluffy. Gradually add the egg yolks, beating well after each addition, then beat in the cardamom.

2 Gently stir the rice flour into the butter mixture to form a smooth soft dough. Turn on to a lightly floured surface and knead lightly several times. Turn the mixing bowl over the dough and let it rest, about 1 hour.

3 Form heaped teaspoonfuls of the dough into balls, then form into crescent shapes. Place 5 cm/2 inches apart on greased baking sheets. Mark a pattern on the tops with a spoon.

4 Brush each crescent with a little beaten egg white and sprinkle with the chopped nuts.

5 Bake in a preheated oven at 350°C/180°F/Gas Mark 4 for about 15 minutes until the bases begin to colour; the tops should remain very pale. Reduce the heat if the tops begin to colour.

6 Cool on the baking sheets for about 2 minutes, then transfer the cookies to wire racks to cool completely. Dust with icing sugar and store in an airtight container.

Chocolate Peanut Biscuits

Makes 50–60 biscuits

INGREDIENTS

175 g/6 oz plain flour	pinch salt	115 g/4 oz unsalted peanuts,
250 g/9 oz rice flour	135 g/4¾ oz white vegetable fat	finely chopped
25 g/1 oz unsweetened	200 g/7 oz caster sugar	175 g/6 oz plain or continental
cocoa powder	1 tsp vanilla essence	plain chocolate, melted
1 tsp baking powder	140 g/5 oz raisins, chopped	

1 Sift the flours, cocoa, baking powder and salt into a bowl, then stir to combine.

2 Using an electric mixer, beat the fat and sugar in a large bowl for about 2 minutes until very light and creamy. Beat in the vanilla. Gradually blend in the flour mixture to form a soft dough. Stir in the raisins.

3 Put the chopped peanuts in a small bowl. Pinch off walnut-size pieces of the dough and roll into balls. Drop into the peanuts and roll to coat, pressing them lightly to stick. Place the balls about 7.5 cm/ 3 inches apart on 2 large greased non-stick baking sheets.

4 Using the flat bottom of a drinking glass, dipped in flour, gently flatten each ball to a round about 5 mm/ ¼ inch thick.

5 Bake in a preheated oven at 180°C/350°F/ Gas Mark 4 for about 10 minutes until golden and lightly set; do not over bake. Cool on the sheets for about 1 minute, then, using a thin palette knife, transfer to a wire rack to cool. Continue with the remaining dough and peanuts.

6 Arrange the cooled cookies close together on the wire rack and drizzle the tops with the melted chocolate. Let it set before transferring to an airtight container with greaseproof paper between the layers.

Christmas Rice Pancakes

Makes about 24 pancakes

INGREDIENTS

700 ml/1¼ pints milk	40 g/1½ oz plain flour	½ tsp almond essence
salt	1 tsp baking powder	2 tbsp butter, melted
100 g/3½ oz long-grain	¾ tsp bicarbonate of soda	350 g/12 oz homemade or
white rice	2 eggs, beaten	bought mincemeat
1 cinnamon stick	125 ml/4 fl oz soured cream	melted butter, for frying
60 g/2¼ oz sugar	2 tbsp dark rum	ground cinnamon, for dusting
	1 tsp vanilla essence	

1 To make the pancakes, bring the milk to the boil in a saucepan. Add a pinch of salt and sprinkle in the rice. Add the cinnamon stick and simmer gently for about 35 minutes until the rice is tender and the milk almost absorbed.

2 Remove from the heat, add the sugar and stir until dissolved. Discard the cinnamon stick and pour into a large bowl. Cool, stirring occasionally, for about 30 minutes.

3 Combine the flour, baking powder, bicarbonate of soda and a pinch of salt; set aside. Beat the eggs with the soured cream, rum, vanilla and almond essences and the melted butter. Whisk the egg mixture into the rice, then stir in the flour mixture until just blended; do not over-mix. Fold in the mincemeat.

4 Heat a large frying pan or griddle, and brush with butter. Stir the batter and drop 2–3 tablespoons on to the pan. Cook for about 2 minutes until the undersides are golden and the tops covered with bubbles that burst open. Gently turn, cook for another minute. Keep warm.

5 Dust the pancakes with cinnamon and serve.

COOK'S TIP

For a Christmas custard, soak 140 g/5 oz raisins in boiling water. Bring 350ml/12fl oz milk to the boil. Scrape the seeds out of a vanilla pod and add to the millk with the pod. Bring to the boil, remove from the heat, cover and stand for 10 minutes. Beat 5 eggs with sugar to taste until thick, beat in half the milk, then return the mixture to the pan and cook until thickened; do not boil. Strain the raisins, add to the custard with 2–3 tbsp dark rum. Serve chilled.

Rice Muffins with Amaretto Butter

Makes 12 muffins

INGREDIENTS

140 g/5 oz plain flour	50 ml/2 fl oz honey	AMARETTO BUTTER
1 tbsp baking powder	125 ml/4 fl oz milk	115 g/4 oz unsalted butter, at
½ tsp bicarbonate of soda	2 tbsp sunflower oil	room temperature
½ tsp salt	½ tsp almond essence	1 tbsp honey
1 egg	60 g/2¼ oz cooked arborio rice	1–2 tbsp Amaretto liqueur
	2–3 amaretti biscuits, roughly	1–2 tbsp mascarpone
	crushed	

1 Sift the flour, baking powder, bicarbonate of soda and salt into a large bowl and stir. Make a well in the centre.

2 In another bowl, beat the egg, honey, milk, oil and almond essence with an electric mixer for about 2 minutes until light and foamy. Gradually beat in the rice. Pour into the well and, using a fork, stir lightly until just combined. Do not over beat; the mixture can be slightly lumpy.

3 Spoon the batter into a lightly greased 12-cup muffin pan or two 6-cup pans. Sprinkle each with some of the amaretti crumbs and bake in a preheated oven at 200°C/400°F/Gas Mark 6 for about 15 minutes until risen and golden; the tops should spring back lightly when pressed.

4 Cool in the pans on a wire rack for about 1 minute. Carefully remove the muffins and cool slightly.

5 To make the Amaretto butter, put the butter and honey in a small bowl and beat until creamy. Add the Amaretto and mascarpone and beat together. Spoon into a small serving bowl and serve with the warm muffins.

COOK'S TIP

Use paper liners to line the muffin pan cups to avoid sticking.

Mini Orange Rice Cakes

Makes about 16

INGREDIENTS

700 ml/1¼ pints milk
pinch of salt
1 vanilla pod, split, seeds removed
    and reserved
100 g/3½ oz arborio rice

100 g/3½ oz sugar
2 tbsp butter
grated rind of 2 oranges
2 eggs, separated
2 tbsp orange-flavoured liqueur
    or rum

1 tbsp freshly squeezed
    orange juice
1 orange, chopped, to decorate
icing sugar, for dusting

1 Bring the milk to the boil in a large saucepan over medium-high heat. Add the salt and vanilla pod and seeds and sprinkle in the rice. Return to the boil, stirring once or twice. Reduce the heat and simmer, stirring frequently, for about 10 minutes.

2 Add the sugar and butter and continue to simmer for about 10 minutes, stirring frequently, until thick and creamy. Pour into a bowl and stir in the orange rind; remove the vanilla pod. Cool to room temperature, stirring occasionally.

3 Beat the egg yolks with the liqueur and orange juice, then beat into the cooled rice mixture.

4 Beat the egg whites until they hold their peaks almost stiff but not too dry. Stir a spoonful into the rice mixture to lighten it, then gently fold in the remaining whites.

5 Spoon the mixture into 50 ml/2 fl oz muffin pan cups, lined with paper liners, filling to the brim. Bake in a preheated oven at 190°C/375°F/Gas Mark 5 for about 20 minutes until golden and cooked through. Cool on a wire rack for 2 minutes, then remove the liners and cool completely. Decorate with chopped orange and dust with icing sugar before serving.

COOK'S TIP

Rinsing the saucepan with water before adding the milk to boil helps prevent the milk from scorching.

New Orleans Fried Rice Cakes

Makes about 12 cakes

INGREDIENTS

100 g/3½ oz long-grain white rice	1½ tsp baking powder	70 g/2½ oz plain flour
1 egg	½ tsp ground cinnamon	vegetable oil, for frying
2–3 tbsp sugar	¼ tsp salt	icing sugar,
	2 tsp vanilla essence	for dusting

1 Bring a saucepan of water to the boil. Sprinkle in the rice and return to the boil, stirring once or twice. Reduce the heat and simmer for 15–20 minutes until the rice is tender. Drain, rinse and drain again. Spread the rice on to a dry tea towel to dry completely.

2 Using an electric mixer, beat the egg for about 2 minutes until light and frothy. Add the sugar, baking powder, cinnamon and salt and continue beating until

well blended; beat in the vanilla. Add the flour and stir until well blended, then gently fold in the rice. Cover the bowl with cling film and allow to rest at room temperature for about 20 minutes.

3 Meanwhile, heat about 10 cm/4 inches of oil in a deep-fat fryer to 375°C/190°F or until a cube of bread browns in about 25–30 seconds.

4 Drop rounded tablespoons of the batter

into the oil, about 3 or 4 at a time. Cook for 4–5 minutes, turning gently, until puffed and golden and cooked through.

5 Using a slotted spoon, transfer to double-thickness kitchen paper to drain. Continue with the remaining batter; keep warm in a low oven while frying the rest. Dust the rice cakes with icing sugar to serve.

Italian Lemon Rice Cake

Serves 8–10

INGREDIENTS

1 litre/1¾ pints milk
pinch of salt
200 g/7 oz arborio or
    pudding rice
1 vanilla pod, split, seeds
    removed and reserved
60 g/2¼ oz currants
50 ml/2 fl oz rum or water

2 tsp melted butter, for greasing
cornmeal or polenta, for dusting
140 g/5 oz sugar
grated rind of 1 large lemon
4 tbsp butter, diced
3 eggs
2–3 tbsp lemon juice (optional)
icing sugar

TO SERVE
175 g/6 oz mascarpone
2 tbsp rum
2 tbsp whipping cream

1 Bring the milk to the boil in a heavy-based saucepan. Sprinkle in the salt and rice and bring back to the boil. Add the vanilla pod and seeds to the milk. Reduce the heat and simmer, partially covered, for about 30 minutes until the rice is tender and the milk is absorbed; stir occasionally.

2 Meanwhile, bring the currants and rum to the boil in a small saucepan; set aside until the rum is absorbed.

3 Brush with butter the bottom and side of a 25 cm/10 inch cake tin with a removable bottom. Dust with 2–3 tablespoons of cornmeal to coat evenly; shake out any excess.

4 Remove the rice from the heat and remove the vanilla pod. Stir in all but 1 tablespoon of sugar, with the lemon rind and butter, until the sugar is dissolved. Place in iced water to cool; stir in the soaked currants and remaining rum.

5 Using an electric mixer, beat the eggs for about 2 minutes until light and foamy. Gradually beat in about half the rice mixture, then stir in the rest. If using, stir in the lemon juice.

6 Pour into the prepared tin and smooth the top evenly. Sprinkle with the reserved tablespoon of sugar and bake in a preheated oven at 325°C/160°F/Gas Mark 3 for about 40 minutes until risen and golden and slightly firm. Cool in the tin on a wire rack.

7 Remove the sides of the tin and dust the top with icing sugar. Transfer the cake to a serving plate. Whisk the mascarpone with the rum and cream and serve with the cake.

Sweet Risotto Cake with Muscat Berries

Serves 6–8

INGREDIENTS

90 g/3¼ oz arborio rice
350 ml/12 fl oz milk
3–4 tbsp sugar
½ tsp freshly grated nutmeg
salt
190 g/6½ oz plain flour
1½ tsp baking powder
1 tsp bicarbonate of soda
1–2 tbsp caster sugar
1 egg

175 ml/6 fl oz milk
125 ml/4 fl oz soured cream or
     yogurt
1 tbsp butter, melted
2 tbsp honey
½ tsp almond essence
2 tbsp toasted flaked almonds
2 tbsp melted butter, for greasing
icing sugar, for dusting (optional)

MUSCAT BERRIES
450 g/1 lb mixed summer berries,
     such as strawberrries (halved),
     raspberrries and blueberries
50 ml/2 fl oz Muscat wine
1–2 tbsp sugar

MASCARPONE CREAM
2 tbsp Muscat wine
1 tbsp honey
½ tsp almond essence
225 ml/8 fl oz mascarpone

1 Put the rice, milk, sugar, nutmeg and ½ teaspoon of salt in a heavy-based saucepan. Bring to the boil, reduce the heat slightly and cook, stirring constantly, until the rice is tender and the milk has almost been absorbed. Cool.

2 Combine the flour, baking powder, bicarbonate of soda, pinch of salt and the sugar. In a bowl, beat the egg, milk, soured cream, butter, honey and almond essence with an electric mixer until smooth. Gradually beat in the rice. Stir in the flour mixture and the almonds.

3 Gently spoon the mixture into a 23–25 cm/9–10 inch well-greased cake tin with removable bottom, smoothing the top evenly. Bake in a preheated oven at 160°C/325°F/Gas Mark 3 for about 20 minutes until golden. Cool in the tin on a wire rack.

4 Put the berries in a bowl, add the wine and sugar. To make the mascarpone cream, stir all the ingredients together and chill.

5 Remove the sides of the tin and slide the cake on to a serving plate. Dust with icing sugar and serve the cake warm with the Muscat berries and mascarpone cream, (pipe the cream on top of the cake, if liked).

Spicy Carrot-rice Loaf

Serves 8–10

INGREDIENTS

225 g/8 oz plain flour
85 g/3 oz rice flour
2 tsp baking powder
1/2 tsp bicarbonate of soda
½ tsp salt
1 tsp ground cinnamon
½ tsp freshly ground nutmeg

½ tsp ground ginger
60 g/2¼ oz cooked arborio or
long-grain white rice
60 g/2¼ oz chopped pecans
70 g/2½ oz sultanas or raisins
3 eggs
200 g/7 oz sugar

115 g/4 oz light brown sugar
115 g/4 oz butter, melted and
cooled
2 carrots, grated
icing sugar, for dusting

1 Lightly grease a 23 x 12.5 cm/9 x 5 inch loaf tin. Line with non-stick baking parchment and grease; dust lightly with flour.

2 Sift the flour, rice flour, baking powder, bicarbonate of soda, salt and spices into a bowl. Add the rice, nuts and sultanas and toss well to coat. Make a well in the centre of the dry ingredients and set aside.

3 Using an electric mixer, beat the eggs for about 2 minutes until light and foaming. Add the sugars and continue beating for a further 2 minutes. Beat in the melted butter, then stir in the grated carrots until blended.

4 Pour the egg and carrot mixture into the well and, using a fork, stir until a soft batter forms; do not over mix, the batter should be slightly lumpy.

5 Pour into the prepared tin and smooth the top evenly. Bake in a preheated oven at 180°C/350°F/ Gas Mark 4 for 1–1¼ hours until risen and golden; cover the loaf with foil if it colours too quickly.

6 Cool the loaf in the tin on a wire rack for about 10 minutes. Carefully turn out and leave to cool completely. Dust with icing sugar and slice thinly to serve.

Index